SCIENTIFIC AMERICAN EXPLORES BIG IDEAS

Truth, Lies, and Technology

The Editors of *Scientific American*

SCIENTIFIC AMERICAN EDUCATIONAL PUBLISHING
New York

Published in 2023 by Scientific American Educational Publishing
in association with **The Rosen Publishing Group**
2544 Clinton Street, Buffalo NY 14224

Contains material from Scientific American®, a division of Springer Nature America, Inc., reprinted by permission as well as original material from Rosen Publishing Group®.

First Edition

Scientific American
Lisa Pallatroni: Custom Book Editor

Rosen Publishing
David Kuchta: Compiling Editor
Michael Moy: Senior Graphic Designer

Cataloging-in-Publication Data
Names: Scientific American.
Title: Truth, lies, and technology / Scientific American.
Description: New York : Scientific American Educational, 2023. | Series: Scientific american explores big ideas| Includes bibliographic information, glossary and index.
Identifiers: ISBN 9781684169511 (pbk) | ISBN 9781684169528 (library bound) | ISBN 9781684169535 (ebook)
Subjects: LCSH: Information resources – Juvenile literature | Media literacy– Juvenile literature | Misinformation– Juvenile literature | Social media– Juvenile literature
Classification: LCC PN4784.F27 S35 2023 | DDC 070 –dc23

Manufactured in the United States of America
Websites were live at the time of publication.

Cover: metamorworks/Shutterstock.com

CPSIA Compliance Information: Batch #SACW23.
For further information, contact Rosen Publishing at 1-800-237-9932.

CONTENTS

Introduction 6

Section 1: Historical Perspectives 7

1.1 Three Historical Examples of "Fake News" 8
By Krystal D'Costa

1.2 The Deep Roots of Fake News 11
By John Horgan

1.3 Unlimited Information Is Transforming Society 15
By Naomi Oreskes and Erik M. Conway

1.4 To Understand How Science Denial Works, Look to History 25
By Naomi Oreskes

1.5 How the Pandemic Remade Science Journalism 28
By Tanya Lewis

1.6 COVID Has Created a Perfect Storm for Fringe Science 32
By David Robert Grimes

Section 2: Why We Fall For Fake News 36

2.1 People Drawn to Conspiracy Theories Share a Cluster of Psychological Features 37
By Melinda Wenner Moyer

2.2 Cognitive Ability and Vulnerability to Fake News 45
By David Z. Hambrick and Madeline Marquardt

2.3 How Disinformation Hacks Your Brain 50
By Brett Beasley

2.4 Why Are Deepfakes So Effective? 53
By Martijn Rosser

2.5 AI-Generated Deepfakes and the Challenge of Detection 56
By Siwei Lyu

Section 3: The Role of Social Media 60

3.1 You Can't Handle the Truth—at Least on Twitter 61
By Larry Greenemeier

3.2 How Facebook Hinders Misinformation Research 65
By Laura Edelson and Damon McCoy

3.3 Russia's Information War Is Being Waged on Social Media Platforms 69
By Sophie Bushwick

3.4 YouTube's Plan to Showcase Credible Health Information Is Flawed, Experts Warn 73
By Grant Currin

3.5 How Fake News Goes Viral—Here's the Math 78
By Madhusree Mukerjee

3.6 Information Overload Helps Fake News Spread, and Social Media Knows It 83
By Filippo Menczer, Thomas Hills

Section 4: The Politics of Disinformation 94

4.1 How 9/11 Ushered in a New Era of Conspiracy Theories 95
By Jason Stanley

4.2 Personality Type, as well as Politics, Predicts Who Shares Fake News 98
By Asher Lawson and Hemant Kakkar

4.3 Liberals and Conservatives Are Both Susceptible to Fake News, but for Different Reasons 101
By Scott Barry Kaufman

4.4 Fake News Websites May Not Have a Major Effect on Elections 106
By Karen Weintraub

4.5 Russian Misinformation Seeks to Confound, Not Convince 109
By David Robert Grimes

4.6 Clicks, Lies and Videotape 113
By Brooke Borel

Section 5: Improving Media Literacy 124

5.1 Misinformation Has Created a New World Disorder 125
By Claire Wardle

5.2 Schoolkids Are Falling Victim to Disinformation and Conspiracy Fantasies 134
By Melinda Wenner Moyer

5.3 We Should Teach Media Literacy in Elementary School 142
By Prateek Puri

5.4 The Psychology of Fact-Checking 146
By Stephen J. Ceci and Wendy M. Williams

5.5 (Dis)trust in Science 150
By Gleb Tsipursky

Glossary 156

Further Information 157

Citations 158

Index 159

INTRODUCTION

There is no evidence Mark Twain ever said "a lie will fly around the whole world while the Truth is getting its boots on." But that won't stop you from finding thousands of websites and social media posts citing Mark Twain as the author of that quip. You'll also find posts online correcting the mistake, but the misinformation flies faster around the Internet than the truth can catch up to it.

The articles in this book seek to explain and understand the role that new technologies, especially social media, have played in spreading information around the world—some of it true and all too much of it false, even maliciously false.

Misinformation is not new to the world, and Section 1, "Historical Perspectives," looks at the role that propaganda and "fake news" have played in the past and how they have shaped our present day. Section 2, "Why We Fall For Fake News," looks at the attraction of misinformation—why we fall for it, why it's so hard to detect, and how it shapes the way we think and act. Section 3 illustrates "The Role of Social Media" in disseminating misinformation, and how some of the key players in social media—Twitter, YouTube, and Facebook—have tried (or not tried) to combat its dissemination. In Section 4, "The Politics of Disinformation," we look at how truth is often the first casualty of politics and war. And the final section, "Improving Media Literacy," looks at how we can improve the ways we decode media messages in order to separate truth from lies.

Technology is neither good nor evil; it's how we use new technologies that can either create a better world or make it worse. Social media and the Internet more generally are no different. Combating the scourge of "fake news" online is one way we can use that technology for the better, but it won't be easy. Truth will need to learn how to get its boots on more quickly.

Section 1: Historical Perspectives

1.1 Three Historical Examples of "Fake News"
By Krystal D'Costa

1.2 The Deep Roots of Fake News
By John Horgan

1.3 Unlimited Information Is Transforming Society
By Naomi Oreskes and Erik M. Conway

1.4 To Understand How Science Denial Works, Look to History
By Naomi Oreskes

1.5 How the Pandemic Remade Science Journalism
By Tanya Lewis

1.6 COVID Has Created a Perfect Storm for Fringe Science
By David Robert Grimes

Three Historical Examples of "Fake News"

By Krystal D'Costa

In the video game *Assassin's Creed*, if your notoriety rises high, enough, the town criers will start to warn people to be on the lookout for you. While your notoriety fades with time, another way out of this situation is to bribe the town criers. Then they simply stop talking about you. News media is storytelling in one regard. We expect it to be truthful but it is always colored by perception from the author or the audience. And it almost always serves a purpose. As such, "official decrees" have a long history of being manipulated. We know this manipulation to be propaganda; its impact can be far reaching and forever alter the course of history. Here are three historical instances in which falsified facts left a mark.

The Donation of Constantine

As the power of the Catholic Church grew during the Middle Ages, conflicts arose between the Church and the European ruling class over control of the states. In a very handy move, the Church produced a document in the eighth century known as "The Donation of Constantine." The document alleged that Emperor Constantine had transferred land and political control to Pope Sylvester I in the fourth century AD because Sylvester allegedly cured him of leprosy. The Church would successfully use this document numerous times to assert control over various regions. It remained unchallenged until the 15th century, when analysis of the document itself suggested that it could not have been written in the fourth century: the document made use of words that would have been unknown in Constantine's time (like "fief") and employed sentence constructs that were uncommon to Constantine's Latin. The Church backtracked a bit and drafted a document that declared its land had been awarded to it by Charlemagne, but this was never published. Opponents of the Church tried to claim civil law and civil jurisdiction, maintaining that even if the document had been true, it would have only been legitimate during Constantine's lifetime but the Church was already deeply rooted in these regions. Interestingly, even after the *Document* had been established as a forgery, some people continued to believe in its authenticity.

A Sanctioned Surrender

In the 1140s, the Hospitaliers of the Knights Templar were granted property in Tripoli that included the Krak des Chevaliers, a Syrian fort. It became a significant holding for the Knights Hospitaliers, who were able to stage raids on the nearby Homs and grow their numbers into a sizable force. This prosperity would not last forever, however. Sultan Baibars had a serious bone to pick with the Crusaders in general (due to their support of the Mongols) and spent his life routing them out of Syria. In 1271 Baibars laid siege to Krak des Chevaliers. As was common to the time, when the threat of Baibars appeared on the horizon, many of the surrounding villagers fled to the fort for protection. They took up residence in the outer ward of the fort. Baibars' siege engines breached these walls first, which allowed the Hospitaliers to flee inward. The siege came to a halt for a short period and culminated with Baibars' men delivering a letter purported to be from the Grand Master of the Knights Hospitaller in Tripoli. The letter granted the Knights of Krak des Chevaliers permission to surrender. It was a forgery, of course, but the Knights did surrender. Baibars spared their lives but seized the fort and converted it into a mosque.

A Bag of Scalps

In 1782, Benjamin Franklin created a fake issue of a Boston newspaper. The main story was quite gruesome: it maintained that American forces had discovered bags of money and goods that appeared bound for the king but included among them were the scalps of soldiers and civilians. The bag of scalps included a letter addressed to the king asking him to accept the scalps as a token of friendship and loyalty. Franklin sent the newspaper to his friends, who forwarded it to their friends and soon enough the story had been republished in other colonial newspapers. There were signs the original document was a fake–the typeface, for example–but these clues were lost in the sensationalism of the information. The public was outraged. In this case, Franklin's "news" added to the animosity directed against Native Americans and helped establish them as non-Americans who could not be trusted nor should be accepted in the new Republic. The story was resurrected at a later date as "evidence" of the depravity of Native Americans during the War of 1812.

These are three examples, but there are countless others. Not to mention the cases where newspapers themselves created news to sell papers–the *New York Sun* was notorious for this kind of behavior and featured a six-part series on fantastic lunar discoveries made by one Sir John Herschel. In all of these cases, there were signs of falsification but they were overlooked under the guise of authority.

The trust we place in the written word hearkens back to the rarity and expense of producing printed material. Words become permanent on paper and take on a life of their own. Handing someone the Donation of Constantine or a letter from a Templar Grand Master has a finality to it. In that vein, there is also something about the sameness of the experience of print. The idea that different people can get a piece of paper that states the same thing is powerful. It's equalizing. It's easy to trust the information in this case because accepting that a huge group of people are being misled is, well, unbelievable. There isn't a way to prevent fake news entirely, but it starts with critical reading and conversations.

About the Author

Krystal D'Costa is an anthropologist working in digital media in New York City.

The Deep Roots of Fake News

By John Horgan

Jill Lepore, like all historians, faces a challenge. Readers of her magnificent new book, *These Truths: A History of the United States*, know how her story ends, so how can she keep us in suspense? She makes our foreknowledge work to her advantage, because she keeps implicitly and explicitly addressing the question, How the hell did we get here? How could a vulgar, mendacious bully who emboldens racists and sexists and xenophobes, who denounces "fake news" and is a fount of it, who embodies crass American arrogance at its worst, possibly become president?

If "whig history" shows the past leading inevitably to our enlightened present, *These Truths* is an anti-whig history. [*See Clarification.*] Lepore sought a balance, she says, between "reverence and worship, on the one hand, and irreverence and contempt, on the other." But she clearly fears for her country, and she cannot offer assurances that all will end well. "A nation born in revolution," she writes, "will forever struggle against chaos." Donald Trump's ascent wasn't inevitable, perhaps, but it certainly isn't surprising, in the light of Lepore's narrative.

Lepore traces our battles over race, gender, immigration, and economic inequality–and over truth, whatever that is–back to their roots. Her title alludes to the ideal enshrined in the Declaration of Independence: "We hold these truths to be self-evident, that all men are created equal..." That line has always been terribly ironic, because from the start this country's commitment to equality excluded women, Native Americans, slaves, and white men too poor to own land.

With the possible exception of Tolstoy's novel *War and Peace*, *These Truths* is the best historical work I've read, the most gripping and illuminating. Lepore is a master storyteller, offering panoramic views of battles over slavery and women's rights and zooming in on iconic figures like Frederick Douglass and Elizabeth Cady Stanton. I can't do justice to the scope of her 933-page epic, so I'll dwell on one strand of it, which traces the effects, pro and con, of mass media.

The Constitution protects freedom of the press, which Benjamin Franklin and others saw as vital to the health of the newborn democracy. At its best, the early press informed readers and hence made them better citizens, but it also deceived, inflamed, and divided. "Newspapers in the early republic weren't incidentally or inadvertently partisan; they were entirely and enthusiastically partisan," Lepore states. "They weren't especially interested in establishing facts; they were interested in staging a battle of opinions." Sound familiar?

Optimists kept hoping advances in mass media would help us overcome our differences. "The newspaper would hold the Republic together; the telegraph would hold the Republic together; the radio would hold the Republic together; the Internet would hold the Republic together," Lepore notes. "Each time, this assertion would be both right and terribly wrong." Samuel Morse, inventor of the Morse code, predicted in 1855 that the telegraph would "bind man to his fellow man in such bonds of amity as to put an end to war." Six years later the Civil War erupted.

Franklin Roosevelt recognized radio's power to influence the public, and so did fascists. In the 1930s the Nazis mimicked the methods of American public-relations firms and even hired them to broadcast pro-German and anti-Semitic messages in the U.S. and other nations. The *New York Times* and other newspapers deplored this propaganda as "fake news."

Television coverage helped turn Americans against segregation and the war in Vietnam, but these moral advances led Richard Nixon and other conservatives to accuse the media of a liberal bias, a charge that stuck. Roger Ailes, a former advisor to Nixon and Ronald Reagan, said he founded Fox News to "restore objectivity" to television journalism.

"Cyberutopians" promised that the Internet would unify the nation. Lepore quotes *WIRED* declaring in 2000 that Americans are "better educated, more tolerant, and more connected" because of the Internet. "Partisanship, religion, geography, race, gender and other traditional political divisions are giving way to a new standard–wiredness."

The Internet, Lepore says, has indeed "accelerated scholarship, science, medicine, and education" and "aided commerce." But it has also exacerbated economic inequality and political instability, undermined traditional media, and fueled the proliferation of countless alternative "news" sites.

"New sources of news tended to be unedited," Lepore notes, "their facts unverified, their politics unhinged... nearly all political thinking became conspiratorial." Social media "provided a breeding ground for fanaticism, authoritarianism, and nihilism. It had also proved to be easily manipulated, not least by foreign agents."

This situation was ripe for exploitation by Trump, whom Lepore calls "a huckster chronically in and out of bankruptcy court but a reliable ratings booster on the talk show circuit." Trump had a knack for preying on the public's fears and the media's desperation for drama.

Lepore blames the left as well as right for the polarization that wracks this country and for the erosion of our commitment to free speech. Liberals have "engaged in a politics of grievance and contempt: anyone who disagreed with them was racist, sexist, classist, or homophobic–and stupid. On college campuses, they passed 'hate speech' codes, banning speech that they deemed offensive. They would brook no dissent."

In a grim epilogue, Lepore reminds us of a new threat to our union, and all civilization: climate change. Average temperatures in Philadelphia, where the U.S. held its constitutional convention in 1787, have risen from 52 degrees Fahrenheit then to 59 today. And yet the U.S. president has dismissed global warming as a hoax and worked to ease restrictions on fossil-fuel emissions. Trump's election, Lepore laments, has "sown doubts about American leadership in the world, and about the future of democracy itself."

In a recent *New Yorker* essay, Lepore remains glum about the media's decline. She notes that good journalism, which is expensive to produce, cannot compete with cheap, sensational fake news. Old as well as new media are chasing clicks to stay solvent. Lepore warns that "legacy news organizations, hardly less than startups, have violated or changed their editorial standards in ways that have contributed to political chaos and epistemological mayhem." Donation-funded outlets such as *ProPublica* do good work, but their influence is minuscule. Although there is "no shortage of amazing journalists," Lepore writes, journalism "is as addled as an addict, gaunt, wasted and twitchy, its pockets as empty as its nights are sleepless."

Since Lepore denies us a uplifting ending, I'll do my best to provide one. *These Truths* shows that, in spite of our backsliding, we Americans have managed to lurch in the right direction, toward the ideal of equal rights for all. We ended slavery and segregation and avoided the extremes of communism and fascism. Women won the right to vote, and gay men and women won the right to live together and marry. We elected a black man president, twice.

I even see an upside to Trump's election. He proved that money alone doesn't determine the outcome of elections. A media-savvy outsider can beat a better-organized and funded political machine. Progressives can do what Trump did, as Representative Alexandria Ocasio-Cortez proved last fall. Trump also teaches us that we can never take our hard-won progress for granted. We have a lot to lose, precisely because we have come so far.

Clarification: Recent examples of whig history include Steven Pinker's *Better Angels of Our Nature and Enlightenment Now*, which depict reason and decency triumphing over superstition and cruelty. "Whig" is an antiquated English term for liberal or progressive.

About the Author

John Horgan directs the Center for Science Writings at the Stevens Institute of Technology. His books include The End of Science, The End of War *and* Mind-Body Problems. *For many years he wrote the popular blog Cross Check for* Scientific American.

Unlimited Information Is Transforming Society

By Naomi Oreskes and Erik M. Conway

It is a truism among scientists that our enterprise benefits humanity because of the technological breakthroughs that follow in discovery's wake. And it is a truism among historians that the relation between science and technology is far more complex and much less linear than people often assume. Before the 19th century, invention and innovation emerged primarily from craft traditions among people who were not scientists and who were typically unaware of pertinent scientific developments. The magnetic compass, gunpowder, the printing press, the chronometer, the cotton gin, the steam engine, and the water wheel are among the many examples. In the late 1800s, matters changed: craft traditions were reconstructed as "technology" that bore an important relation to science, and scientists began to take a deeper interest in applying theories to practical problems. A good example of the latter is the steam boiler explosion commission, appointed by Congress to investigate such accidents and discussed in *Scientific American*'s issue of March 23, 1878.

Still, technologists frequently worked more in parallel with contemporary science than in sequence. Technologists–soon to be known as engineers–were a different community of people with different goals, values, expectations, and methodologies. Their accomplishments could not be understood simply as applied science. Even in the early 20th century, the often loose link between scientific knowledge and technological advance was surprising; for example, aviation took off before scientists had a working theory of lift. Scientists said that flight by machines "heavier than air" was impossible, but nonetheless airplanes flew.

When we look back on the past 200 years or so, the manipulation of matter and energy stands out as a central domain of both scientific and technical advances. Techno-scientific innovations have sometimes delivered on their promises and sometimes not. Of the biggest advances, three really did change our lives—probably for the better—whereas two were far less consequential than people thought they would be. And one of the overarching impacts we now recognize in hindsight was only weakly anticipated: that by moving matter and energy, we would end up moving information and ideas.

One strong example of science-based technology that changed our lives is electricity. Benjamin Franklin is famous for recognizing that lightning is an atmospheric electrical discharge and for demonstrating in the 1700s that lightning rods can protect people and property. But the major scientific advances in understanding electricity came later when Michael Faraday and James Clerk Maxwell established that it was the flow of electrons—matter—and that it could be understood in the broader context of electromagnetism. Faraday showed that electricity and magnetism are two sides of the same coin: moving electrons creates a magnetic field, and moving a magnet induces electric current in a conductor. This understanding, quantified in Maxwell's equations—a mathematical model for electricity, magnetism, and light—laid the foundation for the invention of the dynamo, electricity generation for industries and households, and telecommunications: telegraph, telephone, radio, and television.

Electricity dramatically expanded the size of factories. Most factories had been powered by water, which meant they had to be located close to streams, typically in narrow river valleys where space was tight. But with electricity, a factory could be erected anywhere and could take on any size, complete with lighting so it could run around the clock. This innovation broadened mass production and, with it, the growth of consumer society. Electricity also transformed daily life, powering the subways, streetcars, and commuter rail that let workers stream in and cities sprawl out and creating the possibility of suburban living. Home lighting extended the time available for reading, sewing and other activities. Entertainment blossomed in a variety of forms, from the "electrifying" lighting displays of the 1904 St. Louis World's Fair to cinema and radio. Home electricity was soon also powering refrigerators, toasters, water heaters, washing machines, and irons. In her 1983 prizewinning book *More Work for Mother*, Ruth Schwartz Cowan argues that these "labor-saving" appliances did more to raise expectations for household order and cleanliness than to save women labor, yet there is no question that they changed the way Americans lived.

One of the most significant and durable changes involved information and ideas. Electricity made the movie camera possible, which prompted the rise of cinema. The first public movie screening was in Paris, in 1895, using a device inspired by Thomas Edison's electric kinetoscope. (The film showed factory workers leaving after a shift.) Within a few years a commercial film industry had developed in Europe and America. Today we think of movies primarily as entertainment–especially given the emergence of the entertainment industry and the centrality of Hollywood in American life–but in the early 20th century many (possibly most) films were documentaries and newsreels. The newsreels, a standard feature in cinemas, became a major source of information about world and national events. They were also a source of propaganda and disinformation, such as a late-1890s "fake news" film about the Dreyfus affair (a French political scandal in which a Jewish army officer was framed on spy charges laced with anti-Semitism) and fake film footage of the 1898 charge up San Juan Hill in the Spanish-American War.

Information drove the rise of radio and television. In the 1880s, Heinrich Hertz demonstrated that radio waves were a form of electromagnetic radiation–as predicted by Maxwell's theory–and in the 1890s, Indian physicist Jagadish Chandra Bose conducted an experiment in which he used microwaves to ignite gunpowder and ring a bell, proving that electromagnetic radiation could travel without wires. These scientific insights laid the foundations for modern telecommunications, and in 1899, Guglielmo Marconi sent the first wireless signals across the English Channel. Techno-fideists–people who place faith in technology–proclaimed that radio would lead to world peace because it enabled people across the globe to communicate. But it was a relatively long road from

Marconi's signals to radio as we know it: the first programs were not developed until the 1920s. Meanwhile radio did nothing to prevent the 1914–1918 Great War, later renamed World War I.

In the early 20th century there was little demand for radio beyond the military and enthusiasts. To persuade people to buy radios, broadcasters had to create content, which required sponsors, which in turn contributed to the growth of advertising, mass marketing and consumer culture. Between the 1920s and the 1940s, radios became a fixture in American homes as programs competed with and often replaced newspapers as people's primary source of information. Radio did not bring us world peace, but it did bring news, music, drama, and presidential speeches into our lives.

Television's story was similar: content had to be created to move the technology into American homes. Commercial sponsors produced many early programs such as *Texaco Star Theater* and *General Electric Theater*. Networks also broadcast events such as baseball games, and in time they began to produce original content, particularly newscasts. Despite (or maybe because of) the mediocre quality of much of this programming, television became massively popular. Although its scientific foundation involved the movement of matter and energy, its technological expression was in the movement of information, entertainment and ideas.

World War II tore the world apart again, and science-based technologies were integral. Historians are nearly unanimous in the belief that operations research, code breaking, radar, sonar and the proximity fuse played larger roles in the Allied victory than the atomic bomb, but it was the bomb that got all the attention. U.S. Secretary of War Henry Stimson promoted the idea that the bomb had brought Japan to its knees, enabling the U.S. to avoid a costly land invasion and saving millions of American lives. We know now that this story was a postwar invention intended to stave off criticism of the bomb's use, which killed 200,000 civilians. U.S. leaders duly declared that the second half of the 20th century would be the Atomic Age. We would have atomic airplanes, trains, ships, even atomic cars. In 1958, Ford Motor Company built a model chassis for the Nucleon, which would be powered by steam from a micro-reactor. (Needless to say, it was never completed, but the model can be seen at the Henry Ford Museum in Dearborn, Mich.) Under President Dwight Eisenhower's Atoms for Peace plan, the U.S. would develop civilian nuclear power both for its own use and for helping developing nations around the globe. American homes would be powered by free nuclear power "too cheap to meter."

The promise of nuclear power was never fulfilled. The U.S. Navy built a fleet of nuclear-powered submarines and switched its aircraft carriers to nuclear power (though not the rest of the surface fleet), and the government assembled a nuclear-powered freighter as a demonstration. But even small reactors proved too expensive or too risky for nearly any civilian purpose. Encouraged by the U.S. government, electrical utilities in the 1950s and 1960s began to develop nuclear generating capacity. By 1979 some 72 reactors were operating across the country, mostly in the East and the Midwest. But even before the infamous accident at the Three Mile Island nuclear power plant that year, demand for new reactors was weakening because capital and construction costs were not falling and public opposition was rising. In the five years after the accident, more than 50 reactors planned in the U.S. were canceled and others required costly retrofits. Nuclear anxieties worsened after the 1986 Chernobyl disaster in the former Soviet Union. Today the U.S. generates about 20 percent of its electricity from nuclear plants, which, though significant, is hardly what nuclear energy's 1950s boosters had predicted.

While some pundits claimed the 20th century was the Atomic Age, others insisted it was the Space Age. American children in mid-century grew up watching science-fiction TV programs centered on the dream of interplanetary and intergalactic journeys, reading comic books starring superheroes from other planets, and listening to vinyl records with songs about the miracle of space travel. Their heroes were Alan Shepard, the first American in space, and John Glenn, the first American to orbit Earth. Some of their parents even made reservations for a flight to the moon promised by Pan

American World Airways, and Stanley Kubrick featured airplane space flight in his 1968 film, *2001: A Space Odyssey*. The message was clear: by 2001 we would be routinely flying in outer space.

The essential physics required for space travel had been known since the days of Galileo and Newton, and history is replete with visionaries who saw the potential in the laws of motion. What made the prospect real in the 20th century was the advent of rocketry. Robert Goddard is often called the "father of modern rocketry," but it was Germans, led by Nazi scientist Wernher von Braun, who built the world's first usable rocket: the V-2 missile. A parallel U.S. Army–funded rocket program at the Jet Propulsion Laboratory demonstrated its own large ballistic missile shortly after the war. The U.S. government's Operation Paperclip discreetly brought von Braun and his team to the states to accelerate the work, which, among other things, eventually led to NASA's Marshall Space Flight Center.

This expensive scientific and engineering effort, pushed by nationalism and federal funding, led to Americans' landing on the moon and returning home in 1969. But the work did not result in routine crewed missions, much less vacations. Despite continued enthusiasm and, recently, substantial private investment, space travel has been pretty much a bust. Yet the same rockets that could launch crewed vessels could propel artificial satellites into Earth orbit, which allowed huge changes in our ability to collect and move information. Satellite telecommunications now let us send information around the globe pretty much instantaneously and at extremely low cost. We can also study our planet from above, leading to significant advances in weather forecasts, understanding the climate, quantifying changes in ecosystems and human populations, analyzing water resources and–through GPS–letting us precisely locate and track people. The irony of space science is that its greatest payoff has been our ability to know in real time what is happening here on Earth. Like radio and TV, space has become a medium for moving information.

A similar evolution occurred with computational technology. Computers were originally designed to replace people (typically women) who did laborious calculations, but today they are mainly a means to store, access, and create "content." Computers appeared as a stealth technology that had far more impact than many of its pioneers envisaged. IBM president Thomas J. Watson is often cited as saying, in 1943, that "I think there is a world market for maybe five computers."

Mechanical and electromechanical calculation devices had been around for a long time, but during World War II, U.S. defense officials sought to make computation much faster through the use of electronics–at the time, thermionic valves, or vacuum tubes. One outcome was Whirlwind, a real-time tube-based computer developed at the Massachusetts Institute of Technology as a flight simulator for the U.S. Navy. During the cold war, the U.S. Air Force turned Whirlwind into the basis of an air-defense system. The Semi-Automatic Ground Environment system (SAGE) was a continent-scale network of computers, radars, wired and wireless telecommunications systems, and interceptors (piloted and not) that operated into the 1980s. SAGE was the key to IBM's abandoning mechanical tabulating machines for mainframe digital computers, and it revealed the potential of very large-scale, automated, networked management systems. Its domain, of course, was information–about a potential military attack.

Early mainframe computers were so huge they filled the better part of a room. They were expensive and ran very hot, requiring cooling. They seemed to be the kind of technology that only a government, or a very large business with deep pockets, could ever justify. In the 1980s, the personal computer changed that outlook dramatically. Suddenly a computer was something any business and many individuals could buy and use not just for intense computation but also for managing information.

That potential exploded with the commercialization of the Internet. When the U.S. Defense Advanced Research Projects Agency set out to develop a secure, failure-tolerant digital communications network, it already had SAGE as a model. But SAGE, built on a telephone system using mechanical switching, was also a model of what the military did not want, because centralized switching centers were highly vulnerable to attack. For a communications system to be "survivable," it would have to have a set of centers, or nodes, interconnected in a network.

The solution—ARPANET—was developed in the 1960s by a diverse group of scientists and engineers funded by the U.S. government. In the 1980s it spawned what we know as the Internet. The Internet, and its killer app the World Wide Web, brought the massive amount of information now at our fingertips, information that has changed the way we live and work and that has powered entirely new industries such as social media, downloadable entertainment, virtual meetings, online shopping and dating, ride sharing, and more. In one sense, the history of the Internet is the opposite of electricity's: the private sector developed electrical generation, but it took the government to distribute the product widely. In contrast, the government developed the Internet, but the private sector delivered it into our homes—a reminder that casual generalizations about technology development are prone to be false. It is also well to remember that around a quarter of American adults still do not have high-speed Internet service.

Why is it that electricity, telecommunications, and computing were so successful, but nuclear power and human space travel have been a letdown? It is clear today that the latter involved heavy doses of wishful thinking. Space travel was imbricated with science fiction, with dreams of heroic courage that continue to fuel unscientific fantasies. Although it turned out to be fairly manageable to launch rockets and send satellites into orbit, putting humans in space—particularly for an extended period—has remained dangerous and expensive.

NASA's space shuttle was supposed to usher in an era of cheap, even profitable, human spaceflight. It did not. So far no one has created a gainful business based on the concept. The launch in late May 2020 of two astronauts to the International Space Station by SpaceX may have changed the possibilities, but it is too soon to tell. Most space entrepreneurs see tourism as the route to profitability, with suborbital flights or perhaps floating space hotels for zero-g recreation. Maybe one day we will have them, but it is worth noting that in the past tourism has followed commercial development and settlement, not the other way around.

Nuclear power also turned out to be extremely expensive, for the same reason: it costs a lot to keep people safe. The idea of electricity too cheap to meter never really made sense; that statement was based on the idea that tiny amounts of cheap uranium fuel could yield a large amount of power, but the fuel is the least of nuclear power's expenses. The main costs are construction, materials and labor, which for nuclear plants have remained far higher than for other power sources, mainly because of all the extra effort that has to go into ensuring safety.

Risk is often a controlling factor for technology. Space travel and nuclear power involve risk levels that have proved acceptable in military contexts but mostly not in civilian ones. And despite the claims of some folks in Silicon Valley, venture capitalists generally do not care much for risk. Governments, especially when defending themselves from actual or anticipated enemies, have been more entrepreneurial than most entrepreneurs. Also, neither human space travel nor nuclear power was a response to market demand. Both were the babies of governments that wanted these technologies for military, political or ideological reasons. We might be tempted to conclude, therefore, that the government should stay out of the technology business, but the Internet was not devised in response to market demand either. It was financed and developed by the U.S. government for military purposes. Once it was opened to civilian use, it grew, metamorphosed and, in time, changed our lives.

In fact, government played a role in the success of all the technologies we have considered here. Although the private sector brought electricity to the big cities–New York, Chicago, St. Louis–the federal government's Rural Electrification Administration brought electricity to much of America, helping to make radio, electric appliances, television and telecommunications part of everyone's daily lives. A good deal of private investment created these technologies, but the transformations that they wrought were enabled by the "hidden hand" of government, and citizens often experienced their value in unanticipated ways.

These unexpected benefits seem to confirm the famous saying—variously attributed to Niels Bohr, Mark Twain, and Yogi Berra—that prediction is very difficult, especially about the future. Historians are loath to make prognostications because in our work we see how generalizations often do not stand up to scrutiny, how no two situations are ever quite the same, and how people's past expectations have so often been confounded.

That said, one change that is already underway in the movement of information is the blurring of boundaries between consumers and producers. In the past the flow of information was almost entirely one-way, from the newspaper, radio, or television to the reader, listener or viewer. Today that flow is increasingly two-way—which was one of Tim Berners-Lee's primary goals when he created the World Wide Web in 1990. We "consumers" can reach one another via Skype, Zoom, and FaceTime; post information through Instagram, Facebook, and Snapchat; and use software to publish our own books, music, and videos—without leaving our couches.

For better or worse, we can expect further blurring of many conventional boundaries—between work and home, between "amateurs" and professionals, and between public and private. We will not vacation on Mars anytime soon, but we might have webcams there showing us Martian sunsets.

About the Authors

Naomi Oreskes is a professor of the history of science at Harvard University. She is the author of Why Trust Science? *(Princeton University Press, 2019) and co-author of* Discerning Experts *(University of Chicago, 2019).*

Erik M. Conway is a visiting associate professor of history at the California Institute of Technology and author of Exploration and Engineering: The Jet Propulsion Laboratory and the Quest for Mars *(Johns Hopkins University Press, 2015).*

To Understand How Science Denial Works, Look to History

By Naomi Oreskes

2020 has been a historic year—and mostly not in a good way. Among many things, we saw a historic level of disregard of scientific advice with respect to the COVID-19 virus, a disregard that made the pandemic worse in the U.S. than in many other countries. But while the events of 2020 may feel unprecedented, the social pattern of rejecting scientific evidence did not suddenly appear this year. There was never any good scientific reason for rejecting the expert advice on COVID, just as there has never been any good scientific reason for doubting that humans evolved, that vaccines save lives, and that greenhouse gases are driving disruptive climate change. To understand the social pattern of rejecting scientific findings and expert advice, we need to look beyond science to history, which tells us that many of the various forms of the rejection of expert evidence and the promotion of disinformation have roots in the history of tobacco.

Throughout the first half of the 20th century, most Americans saw science as something that made our lives better. Science had deepened our understanding of the natural world, which helped us to cure diseases, light our homes, and bring new forms of entertainment into our lives. Perhaps most important, physicists helped to win World War II and became cultural heroes. Chemists got their due, too. As DuPont reminded us, we had "better things for better living through chemistry." At General Electric, scientists and engineers were helping to "bring good things to life." These were not just slogans; corporate R&D really did produce products that measurably improved many American lives. But corporate America was also developing the playbook for science denial and disinformation.

The chief culprit in this darker story was the tobacco industry, whose playbook has been well documented by historians of science, technology, and medicine, as well as epidemiologists and lawyers. It disparaged science by promoting the idea that the link between tobacco use and lung cancer and other diseases was uncertain or incomplete and that the attempt to regulate it was a threat to American freedom. The industry made products more addictive by increasing their nicotine content while publicly denying that nicotine was addictive. With these tactics, the industry was able to delay effective measures to discourage smoking long after the scientific evidence of its harms was clear. In our 2010 book, *Merchants of Doubt*, Erik M. Conway and I showed how the same arguments were used to delay action on acid rain, the ozone hole, and climate change–and this year we saw the spurious "freedom" argument being used to disparage mask wearing.

We also saw the tobacco strategy seeping into social media, which influences public opinion and which many people feel needs to be subject to greater scrutiny and perhaps government regulation. In October 2019, Congress held hearings to investigate the role of Facebook in potentially spreading misinformation. In the summer of 2020, a report from civil-rights law firm Relman Colfax suggested that Facebook posts could contribute to voter suppression. Climate scientists have complained that the social media giant contributes to the spread of climate denial by permitting false or misleading claims while hobbling responses by mainstream scientists by labeling their posts "political."

Without a historical perspective, we might interpret this as a novel problem created by a novel technology. But this past September, a former Facebook manager testified in Congress that the company "took a page from Big Tobacco's playbook, working to make our offering addictive," saying that Facebook was determined to make people addicted to its products while publicly using the euphemism of increasing "engagement." Like the tobacco industry, social media companies sold us a toxic product while insisting that it was simply giving consumers what they wanted.

Scientific colleagues often ask me why I traded a career in science for a career in history. History, for some of them, is just "dwelling on the past." But, as the bard said in *The Tempest*: "What's past is prologue." If we are to confront disinformation, the rejection of scientific findings, and the negative uses of technology, we have to understand the past that has brought us to this point.

About the Author

Naomi Oreskes is a professor of the history of science at Harvard University. She is the author of Why Trust Science? *(Princeton University Press, 2019) and co-author of* Discerning Experts *(University of Chicago, 2019).*

How the Pandemic Remade Science Journalism

By Tanya Lewis

When I first heard the reports of a "mysterious pneumonia" spreading in Wuhan, China, in January 2020, I thought I would write a story or two about it and move on to the next big medical news development. As a health journalist, disease outbreaks are not a rare occurrence on my beat, and most do not rise to the level of an international emergency. But the story of COVID-19 would turn out to be unlike anything I had covered before or am likely—I hope—to ever cover again.

Reporting on the pandemic was like building a plane while flying it—at warp speed in a hurricane. The underlying science was evolving daily, so there was no expert consensus or body of established research to draw on. And there were plenty of people willing to exploit this information vacuum, creating a secondary epidemic of misinformation.

Early on, Chinese authorities suppressed information about the virus, and the Trump administration downplayed its threat to the U.S. Testing blunders and shortages prevented this country from recognizing the number of COVID cases circulating within its borders in the critical early phase when we could have slowed its spread. And for months, health authorities said SARS-CoV-2 was spread primarily by symptomatic people through large respiratory droplets from a cough or a sneeze or by contaminated surfaces (remember the now ridiculous-seeming grocery-disinfecting ritual?). That guidance was based on how some other respiratory diseases circulate, but of course we now know this novel coronavirus commonly spreads through aerosols that linger in the air, often exhaled by a person showing no symptoms at all.

At the heart of science journalism is a focus on evidence. But one of the hardest lessons many other journalists and I learned while reporting on COVID is that absence of evidence is not evidence of absence—and that even advice from renowned public health authorities should sometimes be questioned. Take face masks, for example: in the pandemic's first crucial weeks, the Centers for Disease Control and Prevention and the World Health Organization said the public did not need to wear masks (despite the fact that medical workers and many people in Asia use them routinely to protect against respiratory diseases). At the same time, CDC and WHO officials specifically told people not to buy high-quality respirator masks because health-care workers needed them—breeding confusion and mistrust.

At the time, I debated with my editor over whether to recommend that people wear masks, against the guidance of these esteemed health agencies. I resisted doing so, in part out of deference to these authorities and in part because of a lack of published studies that masks—especially non-medical ones—were protective for the wearer. In retrospect, I should have followed the precautionary principle; in the absence of direct evidence, masks were a reasonable precaution to protect against a respiratory virus. That episode highlighted for me just how challenging it can be when the evidence is shifting in real time and even the experts can't keep up. It wasn't until two years into the pandemic that the CDC and others finally started to emphasize the importance of high-filtration masks, which had been abundantly available in the U.S. for many months.

It didn't take long for bad actors to weaponize the confusion to spread misinformation. Patient zero in this "infodemic" was Donald Trump. The former president routinely downplayed the virus's severity, calling it "no worse than the flu." He blamed China, stoking xenophobia rather than urging people to protect themselves and others. He mocked people who wore masks, politicizing a basic public health measure, while promoting baseless COVID treatments. It wasn't just Trump—Fox News personalities and celebrities such as Joe Rogan and Aaron Rodgers have used their platforms to spread falsehoods about the virus and the vaccines. As a health journalist, my job was no longer purely about explaining the science—I now had to contend with politics and human behavior. Actions as seemingly innocuous as wearing a mask or getting a vaccine to avoid getting a disease had become political statements.

There has perhaps been no more consequential or bitter battleground in the U.S. epidemic than vaccines. The anti-vax movement—a small faction but already a potent force before COVID—took advantage of people's hesitancy about the speed with which the new vaccines were developed to spread lies and misinformation about their effects. COVID anti-vaxxers promoted their dangerous claims under the guise of "freedom," never acknowledging that it comes at the cost of people's lives and the freedom to live without threat of a deadly virus. As science journalists, it was not enough just to report the facts and debunk misinformation—we had to engage with the reasons people believe such falsehoods. We learned to use the latest research on how misinformation spreads to try to expose lies without amplifying them and replace conspiracy theories with truth.

All of this has played out against the backdrop of vast inequities in access to vaccines and health care, both nationwide and globally. One of the biggest lessons of the pandemic for many of us has been that racism, not race, explains why COVID has been even more devastating for people of color.

The arrival of new viral variants further complicated messaging. The mRNA vaccines achieved an effectiveness beyond any expert's wildest dreams. But their protection waned over time, and they have been less effective against the highly contagious Delta and Omicron variants, prompting a return to mask wearing and a hastily implemented booster shot campaign. As I write this, Omicron is spreading rapidly and overwhelming hospitals because it is so transmissible. As journalists, all we can do is try to make sense of the evidence as it develops, hope in hindsight we made the right call, and remind readers it's normal, not bad, to update our knowledge as the virus—and our understanding of it—evolves.

Reporting on COVID has fundamentally changed the way I approach science journalism. I have gained a deeper appreciation for scientific knowledge as a process, not merely an end result. I have seen that it is not enough to simply follow the science—that skepticism of authority is warranted even when that authority comes from respected public health experts. And I have learned that science is *always* political—despite what many scientists like to think. These lessons have been won at a terrible expense. But failing to heed them could doom us to repeat this tragedy when the next pandemic comes.

About the Author

Tanya Lewis is a senior health and medicine editor at Scientific American. *She co-hosts a biweekly podcast, COVID Quickly, with fellow senior medicine editor Josh Fischman.*

COVID Has Created a Perfect Storm for Fringe Science

By David Robert Grimes

The explosion of disinformation about COVID has been a defining aspect of the pandemic. Alongside the virus itself, we've been shadowed by what the World Health Organization has called an infodemic. This is widely known, of course, but much less discussed is the role of ostensible "experts" in perpetuating dangerous fictions. Since the dawn of the crisis, a disconcerting number of eminently qualified scientists and physicians have propagated falsehoods across social media, elevating themselves to the status of gurus in order to lend a veneer of seeming scientific legitimacy to empty, dangerous claims. And these bogus claims, like their pathological namesake, have gone uncontrollably viral.

In March 2020, for example, physician Thomas Cowan insisted that COVID-19 was caused by 5G radio frequencies. Although this assertion was both devoid of evidence and physically impossible, this proved no impediment to widespread acceptance, with anti-5G sentiment accounting for at least 87 arson attacks on cell-phone towers in the U.K. alone. The ostensible documentary *Plandemic*, starring Ph.D. virologist Judy Mikovits, ratcheted up millions of views with the central thesis that coronavirus is a planned hoax. Even Nobel laureates in medicine have been culpable; Luc Montagnier's statement that COVID was likely manufactured earned him both the enthusiastic embrace of conspiracy theorists and the enmity of scientific peers who refuted the conjecture as utterly false.

Ineffective treatments ranging from hydrochloroquine to ivermectin to vitamin D and alternative medicine have thrived too, endorsed by a rogues' gallery of doctors and researchers. Even now, as the life-saving impact of vaccination begins to be felt across the globe, a new cohort of impressively credentialed contrarians has emerged, spreading mistruths about immunization. The grandiosely named

"World Doctors Alliance" is a potent example, boasting amongst its membership physician Vernon Coleman (an anti-vaccine activist and author of a book insisting COVID is a hoax) and Dolores Cahill, the once-respected Irish scientist whose conspiratorial proclamations have become a staple of lockdown protests and COVID denialist disinformation across Europe.

In slickly produced videos shared relentlessly online, these fringe scientists are lauded as experts unafraid to speak truth to power. But it is crucial to note that these individuals, for all their formal credentials, extol a narrative completely at odds with reality, readily refuted by public health bodies the world over. These pseudoscientific, conspiratorial claims are archetypal arguments from authority, where a perceived expert's support is used to justify positions unsupported by data. Scientific claims do not derive their authority by virtue of coming from scientists, but from the weight of the evidence behind them. Pseudoscience, by contrast, tends to focus on ostensible gurus rather than consensus opinion. The only authority a scientist can ever truly invoke is a reflected one, dependent on accurately representing the evidence base. If they embrace fringe positions and jettison the principles of scientific skepticism, then their qualifications, education and prestige mean absolutely nothing.

Were these claims merely vapid, that would be bad enough. Yet they are also uniquely damaging to public understanding. Scientists and physicians occupy an extremely trusted position in society, and an imprimatur of scientific legitimacy is a powerful one. This is a trust utterly abused by fringe figures, who present qualifications as a proxy for scientific validity. This is superficially convincing to the point that it does not matter that these videos originated in conspiratorial circles; the intrinsic aura of "science" afforded by apparent experts enables them to metastasize far beyond this odious origin. This in turn casts a specter of doubt over the advice of public health bodies, distorting public understanding by presenting rank fictions in the stolen robes of science.

The rise of pseudoexperts is perhaps symptomatic of a change in how we access information. As we become curators of our own media, the traditional gatekeepers and fact-checkers once implicit in most reporting have been increasingly sidelined. This in turn has made us more polarized and reduced our ability to differentiate fact from opinion. Motivated reasoning, our human bias towards cherry-picking only arguments that chime with that we wish were true, most certainly plays a role. The impositions of COVID are manifold; it is not surprising that fringe scientists are inevitably invoked as sources for those with strong feelings against lockdowns, masks, and vaccination. Even if we are not ideologically predisposed to such positions, these claims undermine public understanding, blurring perceptions of scientific consensus, nudging us collectively toward fear and distrust.

The dark irony is that these fringe figures weaponize the societal trust afforded to science, unduly amplifying their capacity to unleash serious harm. To mitigate this, we need to keep in mind the vital distinction between "science" and "scientists." Individual scientists are far from infallible; they can be fooled by subtle mistakes, haunted by spurious conclusions, or even become so ideologically wedded to a belief they bend facts to fit that preconception. Their motivations are human; they can be seduced by the lure of money, infamy, or admiration. Science, by contrast, is a systemic method of inquiry, where positions are formed on the totality of evidence. Crucially, to be labeled "scientific," ideas should be testable, and those that fail to withstand dispassionate investigation are duly discarded.

For all their qualifications, fringe scientists fail this basic tenet of science, as they are united in their willingness to embrace conspiracy theory when their claims are refuted. Lack of evidence for their position is airily dismissed as a cover-up by everyone from the WHO to the entire medical establishment. But this performative outrage is so much sound and fury to distract from the inescapable reality that their positions are completely contradicted by the overwhelming weight of scientific evidence. This is scientifically reprehensible, and staggeringly irresponsible, conduct.

It is entirely understandable that many are left confused and uneasy by the vocal assertions of fringe figures, but the onus of proof is always on those making grand claims. The history of science and medicine is littered with the hubris of the arrogant and misguided, and mere credentials are no impediment to being wrong; only evidence truly matters. When confronted with the pronouncement of fringe figures, the motto of the Royal Society should always be at for forefront of our mind: "*Nullius in verba*" (take nobody's word for it).

About the Author

David Robert Grimes is a scientist and author of Good Thinking: Why Flawed Logic Puts Us All at Risk and How Critical Thinking Can Save the World *(The Experiment). His work focuses on health disinformation and conspiracy theory, and he is an international advocate for the public understanding of science. He is a recipient of the Nature/Sense about Science Maddox Prize, and a fellow of the Committee for Skeptical Inquiry.*

Section 2: Why We Fall For Fake News

2.1 People Drawn to Conspiracy Theories Share a Cluster of Psychological Features
By Melinda Wenner Moyer

2.2 Cognitive Ability and Vulnerability to Fake News
By David Z. Hambrick and Madeline Marquardt

2.3 How Disinformation Hacks Your Brain
By Brett Beasley

2.4 Why Are Deepfakes So Effective?
By Martijn Rosser

2.5 AI-Generated Deepfakes and the Challenge of Detection
By Siwei Lyu

People Drawn to Conspiracy Theories Share a Cluster of Psychological Features

By Melinda Wenner Moyer

Stephan Lewandowsky was deep in denial. About six years ago, the cognitive scientist had thrown himself into a study of why some people refuse to accept the overwhelming evidence that the planet is warming and humans are responsible. As he delved into this climate change denialism, Lewandowsky, then at the University of Western Australia, discovered that many of the naysayers also believed in outlandish plots, such as the idea that the Apollo moon landing was a hoax created by the American government. "A lot of the discourse these people were engaging in on the Internet was totally conspiratorial," he recalls.

Lewandowsky's findings, published in 2013 in *Psychological Science*, brought these conspiracy theorists out of the woodwork. Offended by his claims, they criticized his integrity online and demanded that he be fired. (He was not, although he has since moved to the University of Bristol in England.) But as Lewandowsky waded through one irate post after another, he discovered that his critics–in response to his assertions about their conspiratorial tendencies–were actually spreading new conspiracy theories *about him*. These people accused him and his colleagues of faking survey responses and of conducting the research without ethical approval. When his personal website crashed, one blogger accused him of intentionally blocking critics from seeing it. None of it was true.

The irony was amusing at first, but the ranting even included a death threat, and calls and emails to his university became so vicious that the administrative staff who fielded them asked their managers for help. That was when Lewandowsky changed his assessment. "I quickly realized that there was nothing funny about these guys at all," he says.

The dangerous consequences of the conspiratorial perspective–the idea that people or groups are colluding in hidden ways to produce a particular outcome–have become painfully clear. The gunman who shot and killed 11 people and injured six others in a Pittsburgh synagogue in October 2018 justified his attack by claiming that Jewish people were stealthily supporting illegal immigrants. In 2016 a conspiracy theory positing that high-ranking Democratic Party officials were involved in a child sex ring involving several Washington, D.C., area restaurants incited one believer to fire an assault weapon inside a pizzeria. Luckily no one was hurt.

The mindset is surprisingly common, although thankfully it does not often lead to gunfire. More than a quarter of the American population believes there are conspiracies "behind many things in the world," according to a 2017 analysis of government survey data by University of Oxford and University of Liverpool researchers. The prevalence of conspiracy mongering may not be new, but today the theories are becoming more visible, says Viren Swami, a social psychologist at Anglia Ruskin University in England, who studies the phenomenon. For instance, when more than a dozen bombs were sent to prominent Democrats and Trump critics, as well as CNN, in October 2018, a number of high-profile conservatives quickly suggested that the explosives were really a "false flag," a fake attack orchestrated by Democrats to mobilize their supporters during the U.S. midterm elections.

One obvious reason for the current raised profile of this kind of thinking is that the U.S. president is a vocal conspiracy theorist. Donald Trump has suggested, among other things, that the father of Senator Ted Cruz of Texas helped to assassinate President John F. Kennedy and that Democrats funded the same migrant caravan traveling from Honduras to the U.S. that worried the Pittsburgh synagogue shooter.

But there are other factors at play, too. New research suggests that events happening worldwide are nurturing underlying emotions that make people more willing to believe in conspiracies. Experiments have revealed that feelings of anxiety make people think more conspiratorially. Such feelings, along with a sense of disenfranchisement, currently grip many Americans, according to surveys. In such situations, a conspiracy theory can provide comfort by identifying a convenient scapegoat and thereby making the world seem more straightforward and controllable. "People can assume that if these bad guys weren't there, then everything would be fine," Lewandowsky says. "Whereas if you don't believe in a conspiracy theory, then you just have to say terrible things happen randomly."

Discerning fact from fiction can be difficult, however, and some seemingly wild conspiracy ideas turn out to be true. The once scoffed at notion that Russian nationals meddled in the 2016 presidential election is now supported by a slew of guilty pleas, evidence-based indictments, and U.S. intelligence agency conclusions. So how is one to know what to believe? There, too, psychologists have been at work and have uncovered strategies that can help people distinguish plausible theories from those that are almost certainly fake—strategies that seem to become more important by the day.

The Anxiety Connection

In May 2018, the American Psychiatric Association released the results of a national survey suggesting that 39 percent of Americans feel more anxious than they did a year ago, primarily about health, safety, finances, politics, and relationships. Another 2017 report found that 63 percent of Americans are extremely worried about the future of the nation and that 59 percent consider this the lowest point in U.S. history that they can remember. These feelings span the political spectrum. A 2018 Pew Research Center survey found that the majority of both Democrats and Republicans feel that "their side" in politics has been losing in recent years on issues they find important.

Such existential crises can promote conspiratorial thinking. In a 2015 study in the Netherlands, researchers split college students into three groups. People in one group were primed to feel powerless. The scientists asked them to recall and write about a time in their lives when they felt they were not in control of the situation they were in. Those in a second group were cued in the opposite direction. They were asked to write about a time when they felt totally in control. And still others, in a third group, were asked something neutral: to describe what they had for dinner last night. Then the researchers asked all the groups how they felt about the construction of a new subway line in Amsterdam that had been plagued by problems.

Students who had been primed to feel in control were less likely than students in the other two groups to support conspiracy theories regarding the subway line, such as the belief that the city council was stealing from the subway's budget and that it was intentionally jeopardizing residents' safety. Other studies have uncovered similar effects. Swami and his colleagues, for instance, reported in 2016 that individuals who feel stressed are more likely than others to believe in conspiracy theories, and a 2017 study found that promoting anxiety in people also makes them more conspiracy-minded.

Feeling alienated or unwanted also seems to make conspiratorial thinking more attractive. In 2017, Princeton University psychologists set up an experiment with trios of people. The researchers asked all participants to write two paragraphs describing themselves and then told them that their descriptions would be shared with the other two in their group, who would use that information to decide if they would work with the person in the future. After telling some subjects that they had been accepted by their group and others that they had been rejected, the researchers evaluated the subjects' thoughts on various conspiracy-related scenarios. The "rejected" participants, feeling alienated, were more likely than the others to think the scenarios involved a coordinated conspiracy.

It is not just personal crises that encourage individuals to form conspiratorial suspicions. Collective social setbacks do so as well. In a 2018 study, researchers at the University of Minnesota and Lehigh University surveyed more than 3,000 Americans. They found that participants who felt that American values are eroding were more likely than others to agree with conspiratorial statements, such as that "many major events have behind them the actions of a small group of influential people." Joseph Uscinski, a political scientist at the University of Miami, and his colleagues have shown that people who dislike the current political party in power think more conspiratorially than those who support the controlling party. Recently in the U.S., a number of unproved conjectures have come from political liberals as conservatives have ascended to control the government. These include the charge that the White House coerced Anthony Kennedy to retire from the U.S. Supreme Court and the allegation that Russian president Vladimir Putin is blackmailing Trump with a video of him watching prostitutes urinate on a Moscow hotel bed.

When feelings of personal alienation or anxiety are combined with a sense that society is in jeopardy, people experience a kind of conspiratorial double whammy. In a study conducted in 2009, near the start of the U.S.'s Great Recession, Daniel Sullivan, a psychologist now at the University of Arizona, and his colleagues told one group that parts of their lives were largely out of their control because they could be exposed to a natural disaster or some other catastrophe and told another group that things were under their control. Then participants were asked to read essays that argued that the government was handling the economic crisis either well or poorly. Those cued about uncontrolled life situations and told their government was doing a bad job were the most likely to think that negative events in their lives would be instigated by enemies rather than random chance, which is a conspiratorial hallmark.

While humans seek solace in conspiracy theories, however, they rarely find it. "They're appealing but not necessarily satisfying," says Daniel Jolley, a psychologist at Staffordshire University in England. For one thing, conspiratorial thinking can incite individuals to behave in a way that increases their sense of powerlessness, making them feel even worse. A 2014 study co-authored by Jolley found that people who are presented with conspiracy theories about climate change–scientists are just chasing grant money, for instance–are less likely to plan to vote, whereas a 2017 study reported that believing in work-related conspiracies–such as the idea that managers make decisions to protect their own interests–causes individuals to feel less committed to their job. "It can snowball and become a pretty vicious, nasty cycle of inaction and negative behavior," says Karen Douglas, a psychologist at the University of Kent in England and a co-author of the paper on work-related conspiracies.

The negative and alienated beliefs can also promote dangerous behaviors in some, as with the Pittsburgh shootings and the pizzeria attack. But the theories need not involve weapons to inflict harm. People who believe vaccine conspiracy theories, for example, say they are less inclined to vaccinate their kids, which creates pockets of infectious disease that put entire communities at risk.

Telling Fact From Fiction

It may be possible to quell conspiracy ideation, at least to some degree. One long-standing question has been whether or not it is a good idea to counter conspiracy theories with logic and evidence. Some older research has pointed to a "backfire effect"–the idea that refuting misinformation can just make individuals dig their heels in deeper. "If you think there are powerful forces trying to conspire and cover [things] up, when you're given what you see as a cover story, it only shows you how right you are," Uscinski says.

But more recent research suggests that this putative effect is, in fact, rare. A 2016 study reported that when researchers refuted a conspiracy theory by pointing out its logical inconsistencies, it became less enchanting to people. And in a paper published online in 2018 in *Political Behavior*, researchers recruited more than 10,000 people and presented them with corrections to various claims made by political figures. The authors concluded that "evidence of factual backfire is far more tenuous than prior research suggests." In a recent review, the researchers who first described the backfire effect said that it may arise most often when people are being challenged over ideas that define their worldview or sense of self. Finding ways to counter conspiracy theories without challenging a person's identity may therefore be an effective strategy.

Encouraging analytic thinking may also help. In a 2014 study published in *Cognition*, Swami and his colleagues recruited 112 people for an experiment. First, they had everyone fill out a questionnaire that evaluated how strongly they believed in various conspiracy theories. A few weeks later, the subjects came back in and the researchers split them into two groups. One group completed a task that included unscrambling words in sentences containing words such as "analyze" and "rational," which primed them to think more analytically. The second group completed a neutral task.

Then the researchers re-administered the conspiracy theory test to the two groups. Although the groups had been no different in terms of conspiratorial thinking at the beginning of the experiment, the subjects who had been incited to think analytically became less conspiratorial. Thus, by giving people "the tools and the skills to analyze data and to look at data critically and objectively," we might be able to suppress conspiratorial thinking, Swami says.

Analytic thinking can also help discern implausible theories from ones that, crazy as they sound, are supported by evidence. Karen Murphy, an educational psychologist at Pennsylvania State University, suggests that individuals who want to improve their analytic thinking skills should ask three key questions when interpreting conspiracy claims. One: What is your evidence? Two: What is your source for that evidence? Three: What is the reasoning that links your evidence back to the claim? Sources of evidence need to be accurate, credible, and relevant. For instance, "you shouldn't take advice from your mom about whether the yellow color under your fingernails is a bad sign," Murphy says. That kind of information should come from someone who has expertise on the topic, such as a physician.

In addition, false conspiracy theories have several hallmarks, Lewandowsky says. Three of them are particularly noticeable. First, the theories include contradictions. For example, some deniers of climate change argue that there is no scientific consensus on the issue while framing themselves as heroes pushing back against established consensus. Both cannot be true. A second telltale sign is when a contention is based on shaky assumptions. Trump, for instance, claimed that millions of illegal immigrants cast ballots in the 2016 presidential election and were the reason he lost the popular vote. Beyond the complete lack of evidence for such voting, his assumption was that multitudes of such votes–if they existed– would have been for his Democratic opponent. Yet past polls of unauthorized Hispanic immigrants suggest that many of them would have voted for a Republican candidate over a Democratic one.

A third sign that a claim is a far-fetched theory, rather than an actual conspiracy, is that those who support it interpret evidence against their theory as evidence *for* it. When the van of the alleged mail bomber Cesar Sayoc was found in Florida plastered with Trump stickers, for instance, some individuals said this helped to prove that Democrats were really behind the bombs. "If anyone thinks this is what a real conservative's van looks like, you are being willfully ignorant. Cesar Sayoc is clearly just a fall guy for this obvious false flag," one person posted on Twitter.

Conspiracy theories are a human reaction to confusing times. "We're all just trying to understand the world and what's happening in it," says Rob Brotherton, a psychologist at Barnard College and author of *Suspicious Minds: Why We Believe in Conspiracy Theories* (Bloomsbury Sigma, 2015). But real harm can come from such thinking, especially when believers engage in violence as a show of support. By looking out for suspicious signatures and asking thoughtful questions about the stories we encounter, it is still possible to separate truth from lies. It may not always be an easy task, but it is a crucial one for all of us.

About the Author

Melinda Wenner Moyer, a contributing editor at Scientific American, *is author of* How to Raise Kids Who Aren't Assholes: Science-Based Strategies for Better Parenting–From Tots to Teens *(G. P. Putnam & Sons, 2021).*

Cognitive Ability and Vulnerability to Fake News

By David Z. Hambrick and Madeline Marquardt

"Fake news" is Donald Trump's favorite catchphrase. Since the election, it has appeared in some 180 tweets by the president, decrying everything from accusations of sexual assault against him to the Russian collusion investigation to reports that he watches up to eight hours of television a day. Trump may just use "fake news" as a rhetorical device to discredit stories he doesn't like, but there is evidence that *real* fake news is a serious problem. As one alarming example, an analysis by the internet media company Buzzfeed revealed that during the final three months of the 2016 U.S. presidential campaign, the 20 most popular false election stories generated around 1.3 million more Facebook engagements–shares, reactions, and comments–than did the 20 most popular legitimate stories. The most popular fake story was "Pope Francis Shocks World, Endorses Donald Trump for President."

Fake news can distort people's beliefs even after being debunked. For example, repeated over and over, a story such as the one about the Pope endorsing Trump can create a glow around a political candidate that persists long after the story is exposed as fake. A study recently published in the journal *Intelligence* suggests that some people may have an especially difficult time rejecting misinformation. Asked to rate a fictitious person on a range of character traits, people who scored low on a test of cognitive ability continued to be influenced by damaging information about the person even after they were explicitly told the information was false. The study is significant because it identifies what may be a major risk factor for vulnerability to fake news.

Ghent University researchers Jonas De Keersmaecker and Arne Roets first had over 400 subjects take a personality test. They then randomly assigned each subject to one of two conditions.

In the experimental condition, the subjects read a biographical description of a young woman named Nathalie. The bio explained that Nathalie, a nurse at a local hospital, "was arrested for stealing drugs from the hospital; she has been stealing drugs for 2 years and selling them on the street in order to buy designer clothes." The subjects then rated Nathalie on traits such as trustworthiness and sincerity, after which they took a test of cognitive ability. Finally, the subjects saw a message on their computer screen explicitly stating that the information about Nathalie stealing drugs and getting arrested was not true, and then rated her again on the same traits. The control condition was identical, except that subjects were not given the paragraph with the false information and rated Nathalie only once.

The subjects in the experimental condition initially rated Nathalie much more negatively than did the subjects in the control condition. This was not surprising, considering that they had just learned she was a thief and a drug dealer. The interesting question was whether cognitive ability would predict attitude adjustment—that is, the degree to which the subjects in the experimental condition would rate Nathalie more favorably after being told that this information was false. It did: subjects high in cognitive ability adjusted their ratings more than did those lower in cognitive ability. The subjects with lower cognitive ability had more trouble shaking their negative first impression of Nathalie. This was true even after the researchers statistically controlled for the subjects' level of open-mindedness (their willingness to change their mind when wrong) and right-wing authoritarianism (their intolerance toward others), as assessed by the personality test. Thus, even if a person was open-minded and tolerant, a low level of cognitive ability put them at risk for being unjustifiably harsh in their second evaluation of Nathalie.

One possible explanation for this finding is based on the theory that a person's cognitive ability reflects how well they can regulate the contents of working memory—their "mental workspace" for processing information. First proposed by the cognitive psychologists

Lynn Hasher and Rose Zacks, this theory holds that some people are more prone to "mental clutter" than other people. In other words, some people are less able to discard (or "inhibit") information from their working memory that is no longer relevant to the task at hand—or, as in the case of Nathalie, information that has been discredited. Research on cognitive aging indicates that, in adulthood, this ability declines considerably with advancing age, suggesting that older adults may also be especially vulnerable to fake news. Another reason why cognitive ability may predict vulnerability to fake news is that it correlates highly with education. Through education, people may develop meta-cognitive skills—strategies for monitoring and regulating one's own thinking—that can be used to combat the effects of misinformation.

Meanwhile, other research is shedding light on the mechanisms underlying the effects of misinformation. Repeating a false claim increases its believability, giving it an air of what Stephen Colbert famously called "truthiness." Known as the *illusion of truth effect*, this phenomenon was first demonstrated in the laboratory by Hasher and her colleagues. On each of three days, subjects listened to plausible-sounding statements and rated each on whether they thought it was true. Half of the statements were in fact true, such as *Australia is approximately equal in area to the continental United States*, whereas the other half were false, such as *Zachary Taylor was the first president to die in office* (it was William Henry Harrison). Some of the statements were repeated across days, whereas others were presented only once. The results showed that the average truth rating increased from day to day for the repeated statements, but remained constant for the non-repeated statements, indicating that subjects mistook familiarity for verity.

More recent research reveals that even knowledge of the truth doesn't necessarily protect against the illusion of truth. In a 2015 study published in the *Journal of Experimental Psychology: General*, Lisa Fazio and her colleagues asked subjects to rate a set of statements on how interesting they found them. Following Hasher and colleagues' procedure, some of the statements were true, whereas others were false. The subjects then rated a second set of statements for truthfulness on a six-point scale, from definitely false to definitely true. Some of the statements were repeated from the first set, whereas others were new. Finally, the subjects took a knowledge test that included questions based on the statements. The results revealed that repetition increased the subjects' perception of the truthfulness of false statements, even for statements they knew to be false. For example, even if a subject correctly answered *Pacific Ocean* to the question What is the largest ocean on Earth? on the knowledge test, they still tended to give the false statement *The Atlantic Ocean is the largest ocean on Earth* a higher truth rating if it was repeated. When a claim was made to feel familiar through repetition, subjects neglected to consult their own knowledge base in rating the claim's truthfulness.

These studies add to scientific understanding of the fake news problem, which is providing a foundation for an evidenced-based approach to addressing the problem. A recommendation that follows from research on the illusion of truth effect is to serve as your own fact checker. If you are convinced that some claim is true, ask yourself why. Is it because you have credible evidence that the claim is true, or is it just because you've encountered the claim over and over? Also ask yourself if you know of any evidence that refutes the claim. (You just might be surprised to find that you do.) This type of recommendation could be promoted through public service announcements, which have been shown to be effective for things like getting people to litter less and recycle more. For its part, research on individual differences in susceptibility to fake news, such as the study by De Keersmaecker and Roets, can help to identify people who are particularly important to reach through this type of informational campaign.

At a more general level, this research underscores the threat that fake news poses to democratic society. The aim of using fake news as propaganda is to make people think and behave in ways they wouldn't otherwise–for example, hold a view that is contradicted by overwhelming scientific consensus. When this nefarious aim is achieved, citizens no longer have the ability to act in their own self-interest. In the logic of democracy, this isn't just bad for that citizen–it's bad for society.

About the Author

David Z. Hambrick is a professor of psychology at Michigan State University. His research focuses on individual differences in cognition and the development of expertise.

How Disinformation Hacks Your Brain

By Brett Beasley

In 2016, Edgar Welch sent a text message to a friend announcing he was "Raiding a pedo ring, possibly sacraficing [sic] the lives of a few for the lives of many." Two days later, he drove 350 miles to a Washington, D.C., pizza parlor called Comet Ping Pong and entered with a .38 revolver and an AR-15 semiautomatic rifle. He fired shots inside in an attempt to investigate what he believed was a child sex ring with ties to top Democratic Party leaders and sent restaurant patrons and staff fleeing in fear. The sex ring was fake news. The consequences, however, were real. Welch left the premises under arrest and later pled guilty to local and federal weapons charges.

At the time of Welch's disinformation-driven rampage, "post-truth" had just recently entered the public imagination. A few weeks before Welch's arrest, Oxford Dictionaries declared it the word of the year. Many people still struggled to understand how a polite, soft-spoken person like Welch could be led so far from reality. But as the disinformation age has continued to develop since then, science has not stood still. It has given us a more detailed picture than ever of the ways that disinformation hacks our truth judgments.

If the picture is detailed, it is also disconcerting. It suggests that you and I are probably not so different from Edgar Welch as we might like to think. Take, for example, what happens when we are subjected to repeated false claims. In a recent study, a research team led by Jonas De keersmaecker found that even those of us who are intelligent, analytical, and comfortable with ambiguity find statements more believable simply because we have heard them repeated.

This phenomenon, known as the "illusory truth effect," was first documented in the 1970s, but it is more relevant than ever in the era of fake news. One might immediately think of Donald Trump, who is a prolific peddler of this type of untruth. *The Washington Post* reported that there are "more than 350 instances in which [Trump] has repeated a variation of the same claim at least three times." In fact, Trump has repeated some false claims more than 200 times–for example, his claim that his border wall is being built. Of course, there's nothing new about this type of huckster's grift. But online environments supercharge it. They give repeated false claims instant global distribution. More importantly, they allow the person making false claims to go on doing so while dodging the pressure (and potential legal repercussions) that accompany similar claims in public or in traditional news sources.

Psychologists say that what makes repeated claims seem truer is their "fluency." Fluency means the cognitive ease with which we process a claim. Repeated claims are easier to represent and comprehend. For that reason, they just feel good. Our minds take this feeling as a cue that the claim is true.

In a recent review of the research, Nadia M. Brashier and Elizabeth J. Marsh identify two additional ways disinformation hacks our truth judgments. One that is closely related to fluency and the good feelings it generates is memory. The information and experiences stored in our memory are powerful weapons in the fight for truth. But, as with fluency, we take our memories as cues, not as the raw materials for forming well-considered judgments. We tend, in other words, to go with "good enough." We often accept claims as true when they only partially fit with what we know or remember.

Additionally, we can fall prey to the "illusion of explanatory depth," a tendency to overestimate our knowledge and understanding of the issues we care about. Research shows that when we do, we are more likely to hold extreme beliefs and to accept fake news as true.

Unfortunately, digital tools may be making our memories even weaker and less effective for judging truth. As Brashier and Marsh point out, "search algorithms return content based on keywords, not truth. If you search 'flat Earth,' for example, Google dutifully returns photoshopped pictures for a 150-ft. wall of ice that keeps us from slipping off the planet." For this reason, relying on the internet as truth-on-demand rather than looking to our memories and acquired knowledge can backfire in serious ways.

Brashier and Marsh also point out a more basic mismatch between our brains and the digital environment: we tend to make truth our default judgment. This is especially true for visual information. As with the other cues we use to form truth judgments, this is a handy and useful adaptation in other contexts. After all, humans lived for millennia in an environment where we could trust most of our senses most of the time. Now, however, we find ourselves in a new information ecosystem, one in which, according to some sources, we will soon consume more false media than true media. When it comes to coping with that magnitude of misinformation, our brains are simply not well-equipped.

Is there anything we can we do to keep our guard up in the post-truth era? We know that simply fact checking claims is not enough. After all, Edgar Welch's "pedo ring" conspiracy theory had been debunked long before he showed up armed at Comet Ping Pong's door.

There are, however, causes for hope. Once we recognize our vulnerabilities, we can recognize many other ways to design our information consumption with them in mind. Along with Emmaline Drew Eliseev, Brashier and Marsh found they could wipe out the illusory truth effect by simply prompting study participates to behave like fact checkers.

One of the most interesting solutions may be a collaborative one. Ziv Epstein, Gordon Pennycook, and David G. Rand have found that crowd-sourced judgments about the trustworthiness of news sources can be surprisingly accurate. They suggest allowing users of social media to train algorithms to spot fake news as a scalable, decentralized solution. After ignoring warnings from friends and trying unsuccessfully to recruit them, Edgar Welch went it alone. Perhaps if we come together to protect against the vulnerabilities we all share, no one else will make the same mistake.

About the Author

Brett Beasley, PhD, is associate director of the Notre Dame Deloitte Center for Ethical Leadership and a term assistant teaching professor of management and organization at the Mendoza College of Business at the University of Notre Dame.

Why Are Deepfakes So Effective?

By Martijn Rosser

Public opinion shifts, skewed election results, mass confusion, ethnic violence, war. All of these events could easily be triggered by deepfakes—realistic seeming but falsified audio and video made with AI techniques. Leaders in government and industry and the public at large are justifiably alarmed. Fueled by advances in AI and spread over the tentacles of social media, deepfakes may prove to be among the most destabilizing of forces humankind has faced in generations.

It will soon be impossible to tell by the naked eye or ear whether a video or audio clip is authentic. While propaganda is nothing new, the visceral immediacy of voice and image give deepfakes unprecedented impact and authority; as a result, both governments and industry are scrambling to develop ways to reliably detect them. Silicon Valley startup Amber, for example, is working on ways to detect even the most sophisticated altered video. You can imagine a day when we can verify the authenticity and provenance of a video by way of a digital watermark.

Developing deepfake detection technology is important, but it's only part of the solution. It is the human factor—weaknesses in our human psychology—not their technical sophistication that make deepfakes so effective. New research hints at how foundational the problem is.

After showing over 3,000 adults fake images accompanied by fabricated text, a group of researchers reached two conclusions. First, the more online experience and familiarity with digital photography one had, the more skeptical the person evaluating the information was. Second, confirmation bias—the tendency to frame new information to support our pre-existing beliefs—was a big factor in how people judged the veracity of the fake information.

The researchers recommend focusing on improved digital literacy to counter deepfakes. While sensible, this is just part of the answer. As a society, we need to go further. Deepfakes work so well because they have large audiences willing to believe and spread them. We often see what we want to be true–a desirability bias.

To understand how a well-executed deepfake could play into desirability bias, consider these vignettes. The first is a video of a high school student that went viral on Twitter in January, 2019. Many saw a smug young man mocking a tribal elder. Others saw a nervous teenager not knowing how to react in a strange situation. This was unaltered footage. What was missing was context–the truth was more complex. People saw what they wanted to see. The second was a video of Speaker Nancy Pelosi crudely edited to make it appear she was drunkenly slurring her words. It rapidly spread over social media garnering millions of views, a preview of the power of political disinformation.

Today's information sources are increasingly fragmented and micro-targeted. It is easy to find outlets for news you agree with and want to hear, and equally easy to tune out what you don't. This plays into the hands of those who seek to disinform. Bad actors can hijack social media to amplify the desirability bias. Psychologists found that repeating the same message boosts the propaganda effect through a process called priming. The more you are exposed to a statement, the likelier you are to rate it as true.

There is a rich body of research on cognitive psychology and decision-making. One of the best works is *Psychology of Intelligence Analysis*, written by Richards Heuer, a longtime CIA officer. This book is a cornerstone for teaching the art and science of analytic tradecraft in the U.S. intelligence community. It also holds important lessons on how to help combat deepfakes and should be part of the foundation for a new educational approach in the deepfake era.

Two of Heuer's key points are that being aware of cognitive biases is not enough. You also have to apply methods that foster higher levels of critical thinking, such as structuring information using decision trees and causal diagrams, and by challenging assumptions.

American high schools and colleges should incorporate cognitive psychology into their mandatory curricula. In an era of constant information and disinformation bombardment, there is a societal need to improve critical thinking by teaching tools and techniques to tackle cognitive biases. While this will not be easy, even successfully teaching a small percentage of students these concepts will help. Teaching people to pause and assess information before blindly sharing a shocking video will help to stem a deepfake's spread.

We cannot look to technology alone to tackle the problem. The reason deepfakes work is rooted too deeply. Our biases enable false media to flourish. In understanding how to spot and address our biases, within ourselves and in others, we stand a better chance of mitigating the deepfake threat.

About the Author

Martijn Rasser is a senior fellow in the Technology and National Security Program at the Center for a New American Security.

AI-Generated Deepfakes and the Challenge of Detection

By Siwei Lyu

Falsified videos created by AI—in particular, by deep neural networks (DNNs)—are a recent twist to the disconcerting problem of online disinformation. Although fabrication and manipulation of digital images and videos are not new, the rapid development of AI technology in recent years has made the process to create convincing fake videos much easier and faster. AI-generated fake videos first caught the public's attention in late 2017, when a Reddit account with the name Deepfakes posted pornographic videos generated with a DNN-based face-swapping algorithm. Subsequently, the term *deepfake* has been used more broadly to refer to all types of AI-generated impersonating videos.

While there are interesting and creative applications of deepfakes, they are also likely to be weaponized. We were among the early responders to this phenomenon, and developed the first deepfake detection method based on the lack of realistic eye-blinking in the early generations of deepfake videos in early 2018. Subsequently, there is a surge of interest in developing deepfake detection methods.

Detection Challenge

A climax of these efforts is this year's Deepfake Detection Challenge. Overall, the winning solutions are a tour de force of advanced DNNs (an average precision of 82.56 percent by the top performer). These provide us effective tools to expose deepfakes that are automated and mass-produced by AI algorithms. However, we need to be cautious in reading these results. Although the organizers have made their best effort to simulate situations where deepfake videos are deployed in real life, there is still a significant discrepancy between the performance on the evaluation data set and a more real data set; when tested on unseen videos, the top performer's accuracy reduced to 65.18 percent.

In addition, all solutions are based on clever designs of DNNs and data augmentations, but provide little insight beyond the "black box"–type classification algorithms. Furthermore, these detection results do not reflect the actual detection performance of the algorithm on a single deepfake video, especially ones that have been manually processed and perfected after being generated from the AI algorithms. Such "crafted" deepfake videos are more likely to cause real damage, and careful manual post processing can reduce or remove artifacts that the detection algorithms are predicated on.

Deepfakes and Elections

The technology of making deepfakes is at the disposal of ordinary users; there are quite a few software tools freely available on GitHub, including FakeApp, DFaker, faceswap-GAN, faceswap, and DeepFaceLab—so it's not hard to imagine the technology could be used in political campaigns and other significant social events. However, whether we are going to see any form of deepfake videos in the upcoming elections will be largely determined by non-technical considerations. One important factor is cost. Creating deepfakes, albeit much easier than ever before, still requires time, resources, and skill.

Compared to other, cheaper approaches to disinformation (e.g., repurposing an existing image or video to a different context), deepfakes are still an expensive and inefficient technology. Another factor is that deepfake videos can usually be easily exposed by cross-source fact-checking, and are thus unable to create long-lasting effects. Nevertheless, we should still be on alert for crafted deepfake videos used in an extensive disinformation campaign, or deployed at a particular time (e.g., within a few hours of voting) to cause short-term chaos and confusions.

Future Detection

The competition between the making and detection of deepfakes will not end in the foreseeable future. We will see deepfakes that are easier to make, more realistic, and harder to distinguish. The current bottleneck on the lack of details in the synthesis will be overcome by combining with the GAN models. The training and generating time will be reduced with advances in hardware and in lighter-weight neural network structures. In the past few months we are seeing new algorithms that are able to deliver a much higher level of realism or run in near real time. The latest form of deepfake videos will go beyond simple face swapping, to whole-head synthesis (head puppetry), joint audiovisual synthesis (talking heads) and even whole-body synthesis.

Furthermore, the original deepfakes are only meant to fool human eyes, but recently there are measures to make them also indistinguishable to detection algorithms as well. These measures, known as counter-forensics, take advantage of the fragility of deep neural networks by adding targeted invisible "noise" to the generated deepfake video to mislead the neural network–based detector.

To curb the threat posed by increasingly sophisticated deepfakes, detection technology will also need to keep up the pace. As we try to improve the overall detection performance, emphasis should also be put on increasing the robustness of the detection methods to video compression, social media laundering, and other common post-processing operations, as well as intentional counter-forensics operations. On the other hand, given the propagation speed and reach of online media, even the most effective detection method will largely operate in a postmortem fashion, applicable only after deepfake videos emerge.

Therefore, we will also see developments of more proactive approaches to protect individuals from becoming the victims of such attacks. This can be achieved by "poisoning" the would-be training data to sabotage the training process of deepfake synthesis models. Technologies that authenticate original videos using invisible digital watermarking or control capture will also see active development to complement detection and protection methods.

Needless to say, deepfakes are not only a technical problem, and as the Pandora's box has been opened, they are not going to disappear in the foreseeable future. But with technical improvements in our ability to detect them, and the increased public awareness of the problem, we can learn to coexist with them and to limit their negative impacts in the future.

About the Author

Siwei Lyu is a professor in the Department of Computer Science and the founding director of the Computer Vision and Machine Learning Lab (CVML) at the University at Albany.

Section 3: The Role of Social Media

3.1 You Can't Handle the Truth—at Least on Twitter
By Larry Greenemeier

3.2 How Facebook Hinders Misinformation Research
By Laura Edelson and Damon McCoy

3.3 Russia's Information War Is Being Waged on Social Media Platforms
By Sophie Bushwick

3.4 YouTube's Plan to Showcase Credible Health Information Is Flawed, Experts Warn
By Grant Currin

3.5 How Fake News Goes Viral—Here's the Math
By Madhusree Mukerjee

3.6 Information Overload Helps Fake News Spread, and Social Media Knows It
By Filippo Menczer, Thomas Hills

You Can't Handle the Truth—at Least on Twitter

By Larry Greenemeier

False information spreads much faster and farther than the truth on Twitter–and although it is tempting to blame automated "bot" programs for this, human users are more at fault. These are two conclusions researchers at Massachusetts Institute of Technology drew from their recent study of how news travels on the microblogging site. Their findings, published in *Science*, explain a lot about how conspiracy theories (as well as misleading and downright incorrect information) drown out hard, clear facts on social media.

False news–which the study defines as either inaccurate information presented as truth or opinion presented as fact–is on average about 70 percent more likely to be retweeted than information that faithfully reports actual events, the researchers found. They analyzed roughly 126,000 news stories tweeted by 3 million people between 2006 and 2017. Accurate stories rarely reached more than 1,000 people, yet the most prominent false-news items routinely reached between 1,000 and 100,000 people. Political news, in particular, spread more than three times faster than tweets about terrorism, natural disasters, science, urban legends, or financial information.

When the researchers used an algorithm to weed out tweets likely posted and circulated by bots, both false and true news continued to circulate at the same rates. Bots did not significantly favor one type of news over the other, which suggests Twitter users themselves are largely behind the disparity between the ways fake and real news spread, says study co-author Soroush Vosoughi, a postdoctoral associate at the MIT Media Lab's Laboratory for Social Machines (LSM).

"Human decision-making influences the spread of false news more than we thought," says Sinan Aral, a professor of management at the MIT Sloan School of Management and a study co-author. Aral says this finding surprised him amid all the recent focus on bots—not just in the media but also during testimony before the Senate and House intelligence committees. "It's important to understand the true impact of bots, because that will affect how we deal with the spread of false news," he says.

Politics might be one motivation for spreading fake news. But a bigger problem may be people trying to make a buck in a social media advertising ecosystem that rewards stories for attracting the most eyeballs, says study co-author Deb Roy, LSM's director. "We're discovering that polarization is a great business model," he says.

For its study, the MIT team perused six fact-checking websites—snopes.com, politifact.com, factcheck.org, truthorfiction.com, hoax-slayer.com and urbanlegends.about.com—for common news stories and rumors those sites had examined. "Then we looked for footprints of those stories on Twitter, including links to stories we investigated that were embedded in tweets, tweets about those stories without links, and photo memes related to those stories," Vosoughi says.

False information is likely more widespread because it plays on salacious or controversial elements in ways the truth typically cannot, according to the researchers. "It's easier to be novel and surprising when you're not bound by reality," Roy says. (Twitter is a source of funding for the LSM, but Roy says his lab is "enabled but not directed or directly influenced by Twitter"). Twitter did not immediately respond to a request for comment.

What About Facebook?

Despite their focus on Twitter, the MIT researchers say their findings likely apply to other social media as well. It is difficult to know for sure, because Twitter is one of the few platforms that shares the relevant data with the public. "There needs to be more cooperation between the platform makers and independent researchers, such as those from MIT," says David Lazer, a professor of political science and computer and information science at Northeastern

University who is familiar with—but did not participate in—the MIT Twitter study.

The ability to investigate more platforms is crucial to understanding the scope of social media's false-news problem. Studies show more people get their news from Facebook than they do from Twitter, but it is difficult to say which site is more vulnerable to manipulation, Lazer says. On Twitter, people are more likely to be exposed to a wider variety of users with different agendas, he says. "On Facebook you have people who are more likely to know one another sharing information, so it is possible the purpose of sharing is less to deceive than it would be on Twitter," Lazer adds. Facebook declined to comment for this article.

"Facebook is clearly the 800-pound gorilla in this conversation, but they have been much less transparent than Twitter," says Matthew Baum, a professor of global communications at Harvard University's Kennedy School of Government. "Twitter matters, of course, and we can still learn a lot by studying dissemination patterns on that platform. But at the end of the day you're going to have to find a way to work with Facebook." Baum says he and Kennedy School colleagues are preparing to also study the potential role of platforms beyond social media, including WhatsApp and other direct-messaging tools.

False v. Fake

Baum and Lazer are part of a team that co-authored a separate article in *Science* about the impact of false and misleading information spread online, and potential ways to intervene against it. Unlike the MIT researchers—who avoided saying "fake news" and called the term "irredeemably polarized"—Baum, Lazer and their colleagues embraced it. There has been much debate over the phrase, "because Donald Trump and others have chosen to weaponize it," Lazer acknowledges. "We share those concerns, but also realize any term describing this problem could be similarly weaponized." Baum adds that, given the inherent ambiguity of the language involved—

including terms such as fake news, false news, misinformation and disinformation–they preferred to use the words that so many people have come to associate with the problem.

Whatever the problem is called, solutions remain elusive, especially at a time when fact-checking sites themselves are often accused of bias. "People don't like to be told that they are wrong, so they tend to find a way to counterargue their points even if they've been debunked–and then attribute bias to the fact-checking site that disagreed with them," Baum says. Another problem is fact checking requires resurfacing false claims in order to debunk them, and people often remember the false information without recalling the context in which they read it. For that reason, Baum adds, "we have to find the best modality for fact checking, including where and how to present it."

About the Author

Larry Greenemeier is the associate editor of technology for Scientific American, *covering a variety of tech-related topics, including biotech, computers, military tech, nanotech and robots.*

How Facebook Hinders Misinformation Research

By Laura Edelson and Damon McCoy

When the world first heard that Russia had used Facebook ads in attempts to interfere with the U.S.'s 2016 elections, computer scientists and cybersecurity experts heard a call to action. For the past three years, we have been studying how hate and disinformation spread online so that independent researchers can build stronger defenses to protect the public. But as we have raced to conduct this basic science, we have met steep resistance from the primary platform we study: Facebook. Our own accounts were shut down last month, another sign of the social media company's rejection of scrutiny.

Facebook wants people to see it as "the most transparent platform on the Internet"–in the words of its vice president of integrity in August. But in reality, it has set up nearly insurmountable roadblocks for researchers seeking shareable, independent sources of data. It's true that Facebook does provide researchers with some data: It maintains a searchable online ad library and allows authorized users to download limited information about political ads. Researchers have also been able to use Facebook's business analytics tools to glean some information about the popularity of unpaid content. But the platform not only sharply limits access to these tools, it also aggressively moves to shut down independent efforts to collect data.

This is not just a spat between a social media platform and the people who study it. The proliferation of online misinformation has been called an "infodemic," which, like a virus, grows, replicates and causes harm in the real world. Online misinformation contributes to people's hesitancy to wear masks or get vaccinated to help prevent the spread of COVID-19. It contributes to distrust in the soundness of our election system. To reduce these harms, it is vital that researchers be able to access and share data about social media behavior and the algorithms that shape it. But Facebook's restrictions are getting in the way of this science.

First, Facebook limits which researchers are permitted to receive platform data and requires them to sign agreements that severely curtail how they access it, as well as how they share it. One example of this problem is the FORT (Facebook Open Research and Transparency) program, which Facebook created for researchers to study ad-targeting data. Despite widely touting this tool, however, Facebook limits the available data set to a three-month time period leading up to the 2020 elections. To access the information, researchers must agree to work in a closed environment, and they are not allowed to download the data in order to share it with other researchers. This means others are unable to replicate their findings, a core practice in science that is essential to build confidence in results.

Many scientists have a problem with these limitations. Princeton University misinformation researchers recently described problems with FORT that led them to scrap a project using the tool. Of specific concern was a provision that Facebook had the right to review research before publication. The researchers feared this rule could be used to prevent them from sharing information about ad targeting in the 2020 elections.

Second, Facebook aggressively moves to counter independent sources of data about its platform—and our team is a good example. Last year, we built a tool we call Ad Observer, a citizen science browser extension that allows consenting users to share with us limited and anonymous information about the ads that Facebook shows them. The extension communicates with our project Cybersecurity for Democracy, sending basic information, such as who paid for the ad and how long it ran. It also reports how advertisers target the ads, an issue that researchers and journalists have exposed as a vector in the spread of misinformation. For ethical reasons, we do not collect personal information about people who share the ads they see. And for scientific reasons, we do not need to—everything we need to know to answer our research questions is contained in public information that we are gathering with consent. Even this limited data about ads has been tremendously helpful for our research, and it demonstrates the necessity of independent auditing of social media platforms. With the data collected by our volunteers, we've been able to identify ads promoting the conspiracy theory QAnon and far-right militias, as well as demonstrate that Facebook fails to identify approximately 10 percent of political ads that run on its platform. And we publish our data so that other researchers can work with it, too.

In response, Facebook shut down our personal accounts last month. This prevents Cybersecurity for Democracy from accessing even the limited transparency information the platform provides to researchers. The company insinuated that its actions were mandated by an agreement it entered into with the Federal Trade Commission regarding user privacy. The FTC responded swiftly, telling Facebook that the platform is wrong to block our research in the name of its agreement with the agency: "The consent decree does not bar Facebook from creating exceptions for good-faith research in the public interest. Indeed, the FTC supports efforts to shed light on opaque business practices, especially around surveillance-based advertising."

Facebook has not backed down from its decision to suspend our accounts, and it has other researchers in the crosshairs. Last month, the Germany-based project AlgorithmWatch announced that it had discontinued a project that used crowd-sourced data to monitor how Instagram (a platform also owned by Facebook) treated political posts and other content. In a statement, AlgorithmWatch noted that Facebook had cited privacy concerns with its research.

So where do we go from here? Of course, we think Facebook should reinstate our accounts and stop threatening other legitimate researchers. In the long-term, however, scientists cannot rely on limited voluntary transparency measures from the platforms we follow. Researchers and journalists who study social media platforms in a privacy-shielding way need better legal protections so that companies such as Facebook are not the ones deciding what research can go forward. There are already numerous proposals before the U.S. Congress and the European Union on how to strengthen these protections. Now it's time for lawmakers to take action.

About the Authors

Laura Edelson is a Ph.D. Candidate in computer science at the New York University Tandon School of Engineering. She studies online political communication and develops methods to identify inauthentic content and activity. Edelson's research has powered reporting on social media ad spending in The New York Times, The Wall Street Journal *and* The Atlantic. *Prior to her current time in academia, Laura was a software engineer for Palantir and FactSet. During her time in the industry, she focused on applied machine learning and big data.*

Damon McCoy is an associate professor of computer science and engineering at the New York University Tandon School of Engineering. He received his Ph.D., M.S. and B.S. in computer science from the University of Colorado Boulder. McCoy is the recipient of a National Science Foundation CAREER award, and he is a former CRA/CCC Computing Innovation Fellow.

Russia's Information War Is Being Waged on Social Media Platforms

By Sophie Bushwick

Days after Russia invaded Ukraine, multiple social media platforms—including Facebook, Twitter, and YouTube—announced they had dismantled coordinated networks of accounts spreading disinformation. These networks, which were comprised of fabricated accounts disguised with fake names and AI-generated profile images or hacked accounts, were sharing suspiciously similar anti-Ukraine talking points, suggesting they were being controlled by centralized sources linked to Russia and Belarus.

Russia's Internet Research Agency used similar disinformation campaigns to amplify propaganda about the U.S. election in 2016. But their extent was unclear until after the election—and at the time, they were conducted with little pushback from social media platforms. "There was a sense that the platforms just didn't know what to do," says Laura Edelson, a misinformation researcher and Ph.D. candidate in computer science at New York University. Since then, she says, platforms and governments have become more adept at combating this type of information warfare—and more willing to de-platform bad actors that deliberately spread disinformation. Edelson spoke to *Scientific American* about how an information war is being waged as the conflict continues.

[An edited transcript of the interview follows.]

How do social media platforms combat accounts that spread disinformation?

These kinds of disinformation campaigns—where they are specifically misleading users about the source of the content—that's really easy for platforms to take action against because Facebook has this real name policy: misleading users about who you are is a violation of Facebook's platform rules. But there are [other] things that shouldn't be difficult to take down—that historically Facebook has really struggled with—and that is actors like RT. RT is a Russian state-backed media outlet. And Facebook has really struggled historically on what to do with that. That's what was so impressive about seeing that [Facebook and other platforms] really did start to take some action against RT in the past week, because this has been going on for such a long time. And also, frankly, [social media platforms] have had cover from governments, where governments in Europe have banned Russian state media. And that has given cover to Facebook, YouTube, and other major platforms to do the same thing. In general, banning anyone—but especially banning media—is not a step anyone should take lightly. But RT and Sputnik [another Russia state-backed media outlet] are not regular media: they have such a long track record of polluting the information space.

What else can be done to fight harmful false information?

One of the things that the U.S. did really well going into this conflict—and why, at least from a misinformation [controlling] perspective, the first week went very well—is that the U.S. government was really aggressive with releasing information about what it knew about the ground realities in Russia and Ukraine. That was really helpful for creating a space where it was difficult for the Russians to put out misinformation about those same things. Because the U.S. government was very forthcoming, it didn't leave a lot of room; there wasn't an information vacuum that the Russians could step in and fill. And then the Ukrainian government has been tremendously savvy in telling the story of the Ukrainian resistance. There are definitely times when it has stepped over the line into propaganda. But in general, it has made sure that the world sees the Ukrainian resistance and the fight that the Ukrainian people are willing to put up. That [helps] people see what is going on and understand that the people who are there fighting are real people who, not that long ago, were not fighters. They were civilians, and now they are defending their country.

I think both of those things are going to be difficult to maintain over time. But if they are not maintained, then the window for Russian misinformation will open. A challenge we are all going to have to deal with is that this war is not going to be over in the next few days, but the news cycle cannot maintain this level of focus on these events. It's shocking to say, but in three weeks' time, you will have hours go by without thinking about it. And that is when people's guards are going to go down. If someone is trying to spread some kind of [disinformation]–maybe the Russians make up some fake Ukrainian atrocity or something–that's when the world is going to be susceptible to that kind of thing. And that's when we're going to have to remember all this stuff of "Who was telling you the story? Do we trust them? How verifiable is this account?" This is going to be part of how conflict is waged going forward. But this is something that is new for all actors, and everyone is going to have to get used to keeping up their ground game in the information war, not just in the kinetic war.

Some people have also pointed out an apparent reduction in other forms of misinformation, such as vaccine-related conspiracy theories, since Russia's Internet infrastructure and payment networks were limited by sanctions. What is going on with that?

I haven't seen a large-scale analysis published about this. That said, there have been quite a few anecdotal reports that misinformation in other sectors has decreased markedly in the past week. We can't say for certain that this is because of lack of Internet access in Russia. The conclusion is not that all of this stuff that had been taken down was sourced from Russia. The conclusion that's reasonable to draw from these anecdotal reports is that Russian Internet infrastructure was a vital part of the tool kit of people who spread misinformation. There's a lot of pieces of this economy that are run out of Russia–bot networks, for example, networks of people who buy and sell stolen credit card information, a lot of the economy around buying stolen [social media] accounts–because Russia has historically tolerated a lot of cybercrime. Either it turns a blind eye or a lot of these groups actually directly work for, or are contractors to, the Russian state.

How can we avoid falling for or spreading misinformation?

The bottom line is that people shouldn't have to do this. This is kind of like saying, "My car doesn't have any seat belt. What can I do to protect myself in a crash?" The answer is: your car should have seat belts, and that shouldn't be your job. But unfortunately, it is. With that small caveat, you have to remember that the most successful misinformation succeeds by appealing to emotions rather than reason. If misinformation can tap into that emotive pathway, you're never going to question it because it feels good, and if it feels good, it's adjacent to being true. So the first thing that I recommend is: if something makes you feel emotional—particularly if something makes you feel angry—before you share it or interact with it, really ask yourself the question "Who is promoting this, and do I trust them?"

What is the most important thing platforms need to do to install metaphorical seat belts?

I think the single biggest thing that platforms should be doing, especially in these moments of crisis, is [recognize they] should not promote content solely based on engagement. Because you have to remember that misinformation is really engaging. It is engaging because of some of those reasons I talked about: highly emotive appeal, things that circumvent reason and go straight to the gut. That's a really effective tactic for deception. So I think this is when platforms need to step up the importance of quality of content versus how engaging content is. That is the number one thing they could do, and almost everything else pales in comparison.

About the Author

Sophie Bushwick is an associate editor covering technology at Scientific American.

YouTube's Plan to Showcase Credible Health Information Is Flawed, Experts Warn

By Grant Currin

When someone searches YouTube for a health-related term such as "COVID-19," most results will now prominently feature content from government agencies and health care organizations that the platform trusts to provide reliable information. The World Health Organization, the Mayo Clinic, and the Children's Hospital of Philadelphia are among the channels the platform has deemed "credible" sources of health information, based on guidelines developed by a panel of experts.

YouTube says the new approach is the first step in a larger strategy. The goal is to provide people with a go-to source of reliable answers to health questions in the same way they currently use the site to "learn how to fix my fridge," says Garth Graham, director and global head of health care and public health at Google and YouTube and an associate professor at the University of Connecticut School of Medicine. Many misinformation and public health experts applaud the undertaking, but some worry the recent changes fail to fully address the complexity of health behavior and the contested nature of medical knowledge.

For example, the new policy does not affect the platform's ranking algorithm, which has become notorious as a source of medical misinformation despite previous efforts to reign in conspiracy theories on the site. YouTube helped spread the rumor that hydroxychloroquine is an effective treatment for COVID-19 and hosted the discredited documentary *Plandemic*, which suggested the pandemic was planned, that vaccines do not work, and that masks "activate" the coronavirus–before YouTube took it down. Instead the videos from credible sources appear in a special section, separated from the ordinary search results selected by the ranking algorithm.

The changes also fail to tackle YouTube's role in the multiplatform misinformation ecosystem, says Joan Donovan, research director of the Shorenstein Center on Media, Politics, and Public Policy at Harvard University. For instance, many viewers access misinformation on YouTube through links or videos posted in Facebook groups or on Twitter.

YouTube has banned content that contradicts COVID-19 information from the WHO or local health authorities since May 2020, and it has removed more than one million videos for violating its policy on COVID-19 medical misinformation, according to a company spokesperson. The new changes focus not on removing misinformation but on emphasizing reliable sources. They follow recommendations described in a peer-reviewed discussion paper that was written by a panel of six experts and published by the National Academy of Medicine last month. YouTube provided $100,000 to fund the project.

The authors determined that for a source of health information, "credibility" rests on three foundational principles. First, the source should provide content based on the best available scientific evidence. Second, it should promote objectivity by taking steps to reduce conflicts of interest and bias. Finally, the source needs to disclose its own limitations and errors to ensure transparency and accountability.

YouTube is using these findings as criteria to identify credible government and health care organizations. Videos produced by credible outlets appear in a special section that the company currently calls a "health content shelf," which appears at or near the top of results for a few hundred health-related queries. (As the platform tests this feature, the special section will only appear for certain users some of the time.) These channels' videos are also labeled with messages that briefly explain why the source is credible. In practice, that means channels owned by select government agencies, accredited educational and medical institutions, and academic and medical journals are competing for new digital real estate on the world's second-busiest website.

These changes mark a "massive development in how the company envisions itself," Donovan says. They suggest YouTube is seeking to become "an important source of information" rather than the digital equivalent to "the free bin at a record store." Some experts, however, worry that identifying and elevating health-care organizations and government agencies will not have the intended effect of encouraging people to view more accurate information.

"I'm just not sure that people are tuning in to YouTube to see more scientists or people who have been determined to be credible or authoritative," says Corey Basch, a public health researcher at William Paterson University. Her studies of YouTube and TikTok reveal that videos produced by official organizations tend to be viewed far less often than content from creators who have earned the trust of communities on the platform. The move also does little to address "not unfounded" mistrust in many of the institutions that have been elevated by the change, she says. Basch thinks the problems run far deeper than access to facts. "Sometimes we miss the point that human emotion and behavior is often rooted in social and emotional factors versus cognitive ones," she says. Graham acknowledges that "people trust sources for different reasons" and that information that does not originate from a "culturally relevant" source is unlikely to lead to a change in behavior. He says YouTube has plans to work with independent creators who make medical content that is engaging and reliable, but he would not discuss the plan in any detail.

Sven Bernecker is a philosopher at the University of California, Irvine, who researches fake news as well as the ways medical knowledge is accepted and put into practice. He says the discussion paper's recommendations, which favor well-established sources, are likely to reinforce already existing structures of power and influence in the medical system. Furthermore, he suggests the paper's emphasis on scientific consensus masks disagreement about what conclusions should be drawn from research and clinical experience. Bernecker explains that its recommendations play into the common narrative that science is an objective means of identifying a single truth.

Even a member of the group that prepared the recommendations suggests that information agreed on by scientific consensus does not necessarily represent objective truth. Panel member Wen-Ying Sylvia Chou, a program director at the National Cancer Institute, says the authors "struggled" with the concept of consensus among medical experts–especially knowing that, historically, powerful institutions have excluded certain marginalized groups and ideas from participating in these discussions. That is one reason why they concluded that credibility should be determined holistically rather than according to a quantitative rubric. "A formal numerical threshold can't be implemented [because it is not] feasible," Chou says. Each of the three principles defined in the discussion paper is accompanied by several attributes the authors developed to help with assessing a source. For example, one of the eight attributes it gives for the "science-based" principle is "synthesizes information from multiple sources, rather than a single source."

It is unclear if YouTube did, in fact, create a strict numerical rubric to determine which organizations would be deemed credible. In a statement to *Scientific American*, a company spokesperson said the process began by using the discussion paper's guidelines to compile lists of organizations. "We are starting with organizations with preexisting, standardized vetting mechanisms, such as health care organizations, educational institutions, public health departments, and government organizations," the spokesperson said. The company checked to see which institutions had YouTube accounts before confirming their choices with the American Public Health Association.

"This whole world of health misinformation has been sobering to observe," says Chou, whose background is in public health. "A lot of our assumptions about communication and human behavior are being challenged. There's a lot more research that needs to be done."

About the Author

Grant Currin, a freelance journalist based in Brooklyn, N.Y., writes about research news and educational media. He publishes the newsletter How Do Ideas Spread?

How Fake News Goes Viral—Here's the Math

By Madhusree Mukerjee

NASA runs a child-slave colony on Mars! Photos taken by a Chinese orbiter reveal an alien settlement on the moon! Shape-shifting reptilian extraterrestrials that can control human minds are running the U.S. government!

What drives the astonishing popularity of such stories? Are we a particularly gullible species? Perhaps not—maybe we're just overwhelmed. A bare-bones model of how news spreads on social media, published in June 2017 in *Nature Human Behavior*, indicates that just about anything can go viral. Even in a perfect world, where everyone wants to share real news and is capable of evaluating the veracity of every claim, some fake news would still reach thousands (or even millions) of people, simply because of information overload. It is often impossible to see everything that comes into one's news feed, let alone confirm it. "If you live in a world where you are bombarded with junk—even if you're good at discriminating—you're only seeing a portion of what's out there, so you still may share misinformation," explains computer scientist Filippo Menczer of Indiana University Bloomington (I.U.), one of the model's co-authors. "The competition is so harsh that the good stuff cannot bubble to the top."

Chances are that in the virtual world, the beauty of a photograph or the persuasiveness of an article do help to spread a "meme"—the term Menczer and his colleagues use for a link, video, phrase, or other unit of online information. The researchers demonstrate, however, that just three inexorable factors can explain a network's inability to distinguish truth from falsehood in memes, even if individuals can. They are: the enormous amount of information out there; the limited amount of time and attention people can devote to scrolling through their news feeds and choosing what to share; and the structure of the underlying social networks. All three conspire to spread some of the worst memes at the expense of the best ones.

Mathematical models for exploring how memes spread on social media networks are known as agent-based models because they require the active participation of "agents," a techie term for individuals. These models originate from an older class of simulations that study how diseases spread through a community. Think of a diagram in which each agent is represented by a dot, or node, and is linked via lines to other nodes, representing friends or followers. If, say, Alice is "infected" by an influenza virus or a piece of fake news, she may transmit the contagion along these links to her friends Bob and Clive by shaking hands or sharing the meme with them, respectively. Bob and Clive could in turn pass the contagion to their contacts, and so on. By fleshing out this skeletal framework, scientists try to simulate how far a meme can spread under different conditions.

"Information is not a virus," however, cautions information scientist Kristina Lerman of the University of Southern California, who was not involved in creating the new model. Whereas we are usually dealing with one flu strain at a time, or at worst a few, the number of memes competing to infect us is staggering. The modelers incorporate this abundance by imagining that each person has a screen on which they view incoming memes. The model assigns a value to the probability that Alice will create and share a new meme–say, a video she has made of her dancing cockatoo–and it also does so for all the possible new memes originating from all other users. Because new memes increase the total quantity of information in the system, these values measure the information load experienced by those viewing their screens.

Another parameter tracks the number of items Alice views on her long news feed before choosing to simply pass an existing meme along to her connections, instead of creating a new one. This parameter serves as a proxy for the attention span–the information that Alice focused on. Once Alice sends along a message, it appears on the screens of Bob, Clive and others, who in turn choose whether to create memes of their own or to transmit one of them from their feeds.

Using an earlier version of this model, Menczer and others at I.U. showed in 2012 that a few memes will go viral even if all memes are equally "contagious"–that is, equally likely to be shared each time they are viewed. The memes in both models roughly follow what is called a "power law," meaning that the chance of a meme being tweeted or otherwise shared a certain number of times decreases as an inverse power of that number. For example, a meme is four times less likely to be tweeted twice than once. "If you look at the distribution of pictures on Flickr or articles on Facebook or hashtags on Twitter–all of these have power laws," Menczer says. Still, memes reaching thousands of recipients are surprisingly commonplace.

In 2014 mathematician James Gleeson of the University of Limerick in Ireland and others demonstrated a mathematical similarity between models of the kind concocted by Menczer, among others, and "sandpiles"–canonical systems for what physicists call "self-organized criticality." If one gently dribbles sand onto a flat surface, it will pile up until its slopes reach a critical angle. A few additional grains of sand may cause nothing much to happen, but all of a sudden yet another grain will trigger an avalanche: the equivalent of a meme going viral. Gleeson's analysis suggests the intrinsic properties of the system, as opposed to the particularities of a meme, are driving virality.

In the latest paper Menczer, Xiaoyan Qiu, and others at I.U. examine what happens if some memes are more contagious than others. They find that if the information load is low and the attention span is high, the more attractive memes prevail. Actual tracking of attention and information overload, obtained from Twitter and Tumblr data, however, indicate that in real life the sheer quantity of information usually overwhelms us. "You don't have to assume that the reason why junk spreads is because people like it or because they can't tell the difference," Menczer explains. "You could assume that people do know the difference, and still the fake stuff would go viral, simply because of information overload."

One key factor influencing the spread of memes is the pattern of connections in the underlying social media network. "Some network structures will promote the spread being fast and others will inhibit the spread," says mathematician Mason Porter of the University of California, Los Angeles. If the simulated network in the competition-driven model is assumed to be random, for instance—meaning the connections are randomly distributed among nodes on the network—no memes go viral. Real social media networks display a roughly power-law distribution of links, however—a feature Menczer and his colleagues incorporate into their simulation. So whereas most of us—each a node on Twitter, for example—have a handful of followers, a few outliers may have tens of thousands. If any of these "superconnected" individuals, or hubs, becomes infected with a fake meme, they can presumably transmit it far and wide.

But U.S.C.'s Lerman begs to differ. In disease models, highly connected people are called "superspreaders" because they help drive epidemics. By examining the behavior of actual Twitter users, however, she demonstrated in 2016 that superconnected agents pass on very few of the memes they receive. This is because they cannot possibly see, let alone read, everything in their staggeringly lengthy feeds. "People who are highly connected are unlikely to see anything that is even five minutes old because it is so far down their feed," she notes. Thus information overload ensures they are less likely to get infected in the first place. In her view, hubs suppress the vast majority of memes but may help to spread the few they let through.

Also playing a role in virality: friends tend to form clusters. So, for instance, because Alice knows Bob and Clive, the latter likely know each other as well, and likely share similar views on many issues. These clusters help establish what social media aficionados think of as an "echo chamber." Most of us tend to see some memes several times, increasing the likelihood that we too will share them. Making matters worse, the contagiousness of a meme—unlike that of a flu virus—depends on how often it has been shared. In a web-based experiment involving more than 14,000 volunteers, sociologist Matthew Salganik, then at Columbia University, and others showed in 2006 that recruits were much more likely to download a particular song if they were aware that their peers liked it.

Such "social reinforcement" can ensure that contagiousness increases sharply once a certain threshold of exposure is crossed. "You see one person post, 'NASA's got slave colonies on Mars,' and you think, 'That's ridiculous,'" Porter explains. "You see a second person post, 'NASA's got slave colonies on Mars.' You see this many times, and it somehow becomes more plausible the more times you see it." And so you share it, too. Several research groups are exploring the intricate cognitive processes that lead to one meme being chosen over another.

Debate persists, though, on the accuracy of the models used in this research. "In general, I tend to be skeptical of agent-based models because there are so many knobs you can tweak," Lerman says. Menczer concedes that any model used in an attempt to reproduce all the subtleties of human cognitive behavior would have many unknown parameters—or "knobs"—which would make their results hard to interpret. But that is less of a problem with such minimalistic models (often called "toy models"), which seek only to explore broad-brush features. "As long as they are very simple, they are useful," Menczer says—because they reveal surprisingly powerful truths.

About the Author

Madhusree Mukerjee is Scientific American's *senior editor for science and society.*

Information Overload Helps Fake News Spread, and Social Media Knows It

By Filippo Menczer, Thomas Hills

Consider Andy, who is worried about contracting COVID-19. Unable to read all the articles he sees on it, he relies on trusted friends for tips. When one opines on Facebook that pandemic fears are overblown, Andy dismisses the idea at first. But then the hotel where he works closes its doors, and with his job at risk, Andy starts wondering how serious the threat from the new virus really is. No one he knows has died, after all. A colleague posts an article about the COVID "scare" having been created by Big Pharma in collusion with corrupt politicians, which jibes with Andy's distrust of government. His web search quickly takes him to articles claiming that COVID-19 is no worse than the flu. Andy joins an online group of people who have been or fear being laid off and soon finds himself asking, like many of them, "What pandemic?" When he learns that several of his new friends are planning to attend a rally demanding an end to lockdowns, he decides to join them. Almost no one at the massive protest, including him, wears a mask. When his sister asks about the rally, Andy shares the conviction that has now become part of his identity: COVID is a hoax.

This example illustrates a minefield of cognitive biases. We prefer information from people we trust, our in-group. We pay attention to and are more likely to share information about risks—for Andy, the risk of losing his job. We search for and remember things that fit well with what we already know and understand. These biases are products of our evolutionary past, and for tens of thousands of years, they served us well. People who behaved in accordance with them—for example, by staying away from the overgrown pond bank where someone said there was a viper—were more likely to survive than those who did not.

Modern technologies are amplifying these biases in harmful ways, however. Search engines direct Andy to sites that inflame his suspicions, and social media connects him with like-minded people, feeding his fears. Making matters worse, bots–automated social media accounts that impersonate humans–enable misguided or malevolent actors to take advantage of his vulnerabilities.

Compounding the problem is the proliferation of online information. Viewing and producing blogs, videos, tweets, and other units of information called memes has become so cheap and easy that the information marketplace is inundated. Unable to process all this material, we let our cognitive biases decide what we should pay attention to. These mental shortcuts influence which information we search for, comprehend, remember, and repeat to a harmful extent.

The need to understand these cognitive vulnerabilities and how algorithms use or manipulate them has become urgent. At the University of Warwick in England and at Indiana University Bloomington's Observatory on Social Media (OSoMe, pronounced "awesome"), our teams are using cognitive experiments, simulations, data mining, and artificial intelligence to comprehend the cognitive vulnerabilities of social media users. Insights from psychological studies on the evolution of information conducted at Warwick inform the computer models developed at Indiana, and vice versa. We are also developing analytical and machine-learning aids to fight social media manipulation. Some of these tools are already being used by journalists, civil-society organizations, and individuals to detect inauthentic actors, map the spread of false narratives, and foster news literacy.

Information Overload

The glut of information has generated intense competition for people's attention. As Nobel Prize–winning economist and psychologist Herbert A. Simon noted, "What information consumes is rather obvious: it consumes the attention of its recipients." One of the first consequences of the so-called attention economy is the loss of high-quality information. The OSoMe team demonstrated this result with a set of simple simulations. It represented users of social media such as Andy, called agents, as nodes in a network of online acquaintances. At each time step in the simulation, an agent may either create a meme or reshare one that they see in a news feed. To mimic limited attention, agents are allowed to view only a certain number of items near the top of their news feeds.

Running this simulation over many time steps, Lilian Weng of OSoMe found that as agents' attention became increasingly limited, the propagation of memes came to reflect the power-law distribution of actual social media: the probability that a meme would be shared a given number of times was roughly an inverse power of that number. For example, the likelihood of a meme being shared three times was approximately nine times less than that of its being shared once.

This winner-take-all popularity pattern of memes, in which most are barely noticed while a few spread widely, could not be explained by some of them being more catchy or somehow more valuable: the memes in this simulated world had no intrinsic quality. Virality resulted purely from the statistical consequences of information proliferation in a social network of agents with limited attention. Even when agents preferentially shared memes of higher quality, researcher Xiaoyan Qiu, then at OSoMe, observed little improvement in the overall quality of those shared the most. Our models revealed that even when we want to see and share high-quality information, our inability to view everything in our news feeds inevitably leads us to share things that are partly or completely untrue.

Cognitive biases greatly worsen the problem. In a set of groundbreaking studies in 1932, psychologist Frederic Bartlett told volunteers a Native American legend about a young man who hears war cries and, pursuing them, enters a dreamlike battle that eventually leads to his real death. Bartlett asked the volunteers, who were non-Native, to recall the rather confusing story at increasing intervals, from minutes to years later. He found that as time passed, the rememberers tended to distort the tale's culturally unfamiliar parts such that they were either lost to memory or transformed into more familiar things. We now know that our minds do this all the time: they adjust our understanding of new information so that it fits in with what we already know. One consequence of this so-called confirmation bias is that people often seek out, recall, and understand information that best confirms what they already believe.

This tendency is extremely difficult to correct. Experiments consistently show that even when people encounter balanced information containing views from differing perspectives, they tend to find supporting evidence for what they already believe. And when people with divergent beliefs about emotionally charged issues such as climate change are shown the same information on these topics, they become even more committed to their original positions.

Making matters worse, search engines and social media platforms provide personalized recommendations based on the vast amounts of data they have about users' past preferences. They prioritize information in our feeds that we are most likely to agree with–no matter how fringe–and shield us from information that might change our minds. This makes us easy targets for polarization. Nir Grinberg and his coworkers at Northeastern University recently showed that conservatives in the U.S. are more receptive to misinformation. But our own analysis of consumption of low-quality information on Twitter shows that the vulnerability applies to both sides of the political spectrum, and no one can fully avoid it. Even our ability to detect online manipulation is affected by our political bias, though not symmetrically: Republican users are more likely to mistake bots promoting conservative ideas for humans, whereas Democrats are more likely to mistake conservative human users for bots.

Social Herding

In New York City in August 2019, people began running away from what sounded like gunshots. Others followed, some shouting, "Shooter!" Only later did they learn that the blasts came from a backfiring motorcycle. In such a situation, it may pay to run first and ask questions later. In the absence of clear signals, our brains use information about the crowd to infer appropriate actions, similar to the behavior of schooling fish and flocking birds.

Such social conformity is pervasive. In a fascinating 2006 study involving 14,000 web-based volunteers, Matthew Salganik, then at Columbia University, and his colleagues found that when people can see what music others are downloading, they end up downloading similar songs. Moreover, when people were isolated into "social" groups, in which they could see the preferences of others in their circle but had no information about outsiders, the choices of individual groups rapidly diverged. But the preferences of "nonsocial" groups, where no one knew about others' choices, stayed relatively stable. In other words, social groups create a pressure toward conformity so powerful that it can overcome individual preferences, and by amplifying random early differences, it can cause segregated groups to diverge to extremes.

Social media follows a similar dynamic. We confuse popularity with quality and end up copying the behavior we observe. Experiments on Twitter by Bjarke Mønsted and his colleagues at the Technical University of Denmark and the University of Southern California indicate that information is transmitted via "complex contagion": when we are repeatedly exposed to an idea, typically from many sources, we are more likely to adopt and reshare it. This social bias is further amplified by what psychologists call the "mere exposure" effect: when people are repeatedly exposed to the same stimuli, such as certain faces, they grow to like those stimuli more than those they have encountered less often.

Such biases translate into an irresistible urge to pay attention to information that is going viral—if everybody else is talking about it, it must be important. In addition to showing us items that conform with our views, social media platforms such as Facebook, Twitter, YouTube, and Instagram place popular content at the top of our screens and show us how many people have liked and shared something. Few of us realize that these cues do not provide independent assessments of quality.

In fact, programmers who design the algorithms for ranking memes on social media assume that the "wisdom of crowds" will quickly identify high-quality items; they use popularity as a proxy for quality. Our analysis of vast amounts of anonymous data about clicks shows that all platforms–social media, search engines, and news sites–preferentially serve up information from a narrow subset of popular sources.

To understand why, we modeled how they combine signals for quality and popularity in their rankings. In this model, agents with limited attention–those who see only a given number of items at the top of their news feeds–are also more likely to click on memes ranked higher by the platform. Each item has intrinsic quality, as well as a level of popularity determined by how many times it has been clicked on. Another variable tracks the extent to which the ranking relies on popularity rather than quality. Simulations of this model reveal that such algorithmic bias typically suppresses the quality of memes even in the absence of human bias. Even when we want to share the best information, the algorithms end up misleading us.

Echo Chambers

Most of us do not believe we follow the herd. But our confirmation bias leads us to follow others who are like us, a dynamic that is sometimes referred to as homophily–a tendency for like-minded people to connect with one another. Social media amplifies homophily by allowing users to alter their social network structures through following, unfriending, and so on. The result is that people become segregated into large, dense, and increasingly misinformed communities commonly described as echo chambers.

At OSoMe, we explored the emergence of online echo chambers through another simulation, EchoDemo. In this model, each agent has a political opinion represented by a number ranging from −1 (say, liberal) to +1 (conservative). These inclinations are reflected in agents' posts. Agents are also influenced by the opinions they see in their news feeds, and they can unfollow users with dissimilar opinions. Starting with random initial networks and opinions, we found that the combination of social influence and unfollowing greatly accelerates the formation of polarized and segregated communities.

Indeed, the political echo chambers on Twitter are so extreme that individual users' political leanings can be predicted with high accuracy: you have the same opinions as the majority of your connections. This chambered structure efficiently spreads information within a community while insulating that community from other groups. In 2014 our research group was targeted by a disinformation campaign claiming that we were part of a politically motivated effort to suppress free speech. This false charge spread virally mostly in the conservative echo chamber, whereas debunking articles by fact-checkers were found mainly in the liberal community. Sadly, such segregation of fake news items from their fact-check reports is the norm.

Social media can also increase our negativity. In a recent laboratory study, Robert Jagiello, also at Warwick, found that socially shared information not only bolsters our biases but also becomes more resilient to correction. He investigated how information is passed from person to person in a so-called social diffusion chain. In the experiment, the first person in the chain read a set of articles about either nuclear power or food additives. The articles were designed to be balanced, containing as much positive information (for example, about less carbon pollution or longer-lasting food) as negative information (such as risk of meltdown or possible harm to health).

The first person in the social diffusion chain told the next person about the articles, the second told the third, and so on. We observed an overall increase in the amount of negative information as it passed along the chain—known as the social amplification of risk. Moreover, work by Danielle J. Navarro and her colleagues at the University of New South Wales in Australia found that information in social diffusion chains is most susceptible to distortion by individuals with the most extreme biases.

Even worse, social diffusion also makes negative information more "sticky." When Jagiello subsequently exposed people in the social diffusion chains to the original, balanced information—that is, the news that the first person in the chain had seen—the balanced information did little to reduce individuals' negative attitudes. The information that had passed through people not only had become more negative but also was more resistant to updating.

A 2015 study by OSoMe researchers Emilio Ferrara and Zeyao Yang analyzed empirical data about such "emotional contagion" on Twitter and found that people overexposed to negative content tend to then share negative posts, whereas those overexposed to positive content tend to share more positive posts. Because negative content spreads faster than positive content, it is easy to manipulate emotions by creating narratives that trigger negative responses such as fear and anxiety. Ferrara, now at the University of Southern California, and his colleagues at the Bruno Kessler Foundation in Italy have shown that during Spain's 2017 referendum on Catalan independence, social bots were leveraged to retweet violent and inflammatory narratives, increasing their exposure and exacerbating social conflict.

Rise of the Bots

Information quality is further impaired by social bots, which can exploit all our cognitive loopholes. Bots are easy to create. Social media platforms provide so-called application programming interfaces that make it fairly trivial for a single actor to set up and control thousands of bots. But amplifying a message, even with just a few early upvotes by bots on social media platforms such as Reddit, can have a huge impact on the subsequent popularity of a post.

At OSoMe, we have developed machine-learning algorithms to detect social bots. One of these, Botometer, is a public tool that extracts 1,200 features from a given Twitter account to characterize its profile, friends, social network structure, temporal activity patterns, language and other features. The program compares these characteristics with those of tens of thousands of previously identified bots to give the Twitter account a score for its likely use of automation.

In 2017 we estimated that up to 15 percent of active Twitter accounts were bots–and that they had played a key role in the spread of misinformation during the 2016 U.S. election period. Within seconds of a fake news article being posted–such as one claiming the Clinton campaign was involved in occult rituals–it would be tweeted by many bots, and humans, beguiled by the apparent popularity of the content, would retweet it.

Bots also influence us by pretending to represent people from our in-group. A bot only has to follow, like and retweet someone in an online community to quickly infiltrate it. OSoMe researcher Xiaodan Lou developed another model in which some of the agents are bots that infiltrate a social network and share deceptively engaging low-quality content–think of clickbait. One parameter in the model describes the probability that an authentic agent will follow bots–which, for the purposes of this model, we define as agents that generate memes of zero quality and retweet only one another. Our simulations show that these bots can effectively suppress the entire ecosystem's information quality by infiltrating only a small fraction of the network. Bots can also accelerate the formation of echo chambers by suggesting other inauthentic accounts to be followed, a technique known as creating "follow trains."

Some manipulators play both sides of a divide through separate fake news sites and bots, driving political polarization or monetization by ads. At OSoMe, we recently uncovered a network of inauthentic accounts on Twitter that were all coordinated by the same entity. Some pretended to be pro-Trump supporters of the Make America Great Again campaign, whereas others posed as Trump "resisters"; all asked for political donations. Such operations amplify content that preys on confirmation biases and accelerate the formation of polarized echo chambers.

Curbing Online Manipulation

Understanding our cognitive biases and how algorithms and bots exploit them allows us to better guard against manipulation. OSoMe has produced a number of tools to help people understand their own vulnerabilities, as well as the weaknesses of social media platforms.

One is a mobile app called Fakey that helps users learn how to spot misinformation. The game simulates a social media news feed, showing actual articles from low- and high-credibility sources. Users must decide what they can or should not share and what to fact-check. Analysis of data from Fakey confirms the prevalence of online social herding: users are more likely to share low-credibility articles when they believe that many other people have shared them.

Another program available to the public, called Hoaxy, shows how any extant meme spreads through Twitter. In this visualization, nodes represent actual Twitter accounts, and links depict how retweets, quotes, mentions, and replies propagate the meme from account to account. Each node has a color representing its score from Botometer, which allows users to see the scale at which bots amplify misinformation. These tools have been used by investigative journalists to uncover the roots of misinformation campaigns, such as one pushing the "pizzagate" conspiracy in the U.S. They also helped to detect bot-driven voter-suppression efforts during the 2018 U.S. midterm election. Manipulation is getting harder to spot, however, as machine-learning algorithms become better at emulating human behavior.

Apart from spreading fake news, misinformation campaigns can also divert attention from other, more serious problems. To combat such manipulation, we have recently developed a software tool called BotSlayer. It extracts hashtags, links, accounts, and other features that co-occur in tweets about topics a user wishes to study. For each entity, BotSlayer tracks the tweets, the accounts posting them, and their bot scores to flag entities that are trending and probably being amplified by bots or coordinated accounts. The goal is to enable reporters, civil-society organizations, and political candidates to spot and track inauthentic influence campaigns in real time.

These programmatic tools are important aids, but institutional changes are also necessary to curb the proliferation of fake news. Education can help, although it is unlikely to encompass all the topics on which people are misled. Some governments and social media platforms are also trying to clamp down on online manipulation and fake news. But who decides what is fake or manipulative and what is not? Information can come with warning labels such as the ones Facebook and Twitter have started providing, but can the people who apply those labels be trusted? The risk that such measures could deliberately or inadvertently suppress free speech, which is vital for robust democracies, is real. The dominance of social media platforms with global reach and close ties with governments further complicates the possibilities.

One of the best ideas may be to make it more difficult to create and share low-quality information. This could involve adding friction by forcing people to pay to share or receive information. Payment could be in the form of time, mental work such as puzzles, or microscopic fees for subscriptions or usage. Automated posting should be treated like advertising. Some platforms are already using friction in the form of CAPTCHAs and phone confirmation to access accounts. Twitter has placed limits on automated posting. These efforts could be expanded to gradually shift online sharing incentives toward information that is valuable to consumers.

Free communication is not free. By decreasing the cost of information, we have decreased its value and invited its adulteration. To restore the health of our information ecosystem, we must understand the vulnerabilities of our overwhelmed minds and how the economics of information can be leveraged to protect us from being misled.

About the Authors

Filippo Menczer is the Luddy Distinguished Professor of Informatics and Computer Science, at Indiana University.

Thomas Hills is a professor of psychology and director of the Behavioral and Data Science master's program at the University of Warwick in England. His research addresses the evolution of mind and information.

Section 4: The Politics of Disinformation

4.1 How 9/11 Ushered in a New Era of Conspiracy Theories
By Jason Stanley

4.2 Personality Type, as well as Politics, Predicts Who Shares Fake News
By Asher Lawson and Hemant Kakkar

4.3 Liberals and Conservatives Are Both Susceptible to Fake News, but for Different Reasons
By Scott Barry Kaufman

4.4 Fake News Websites May Not Have a Major Effect on Elections
By Karen Weintraub

4.5 Russian Misinformation Seeks to Confound, Not Convince
By David Robert Grimes

4.6 Clicks, Lies, and Videotape
By Brooke Borel

How 9/11 Ushered in a New Era of Conspiracy Theories

By Jason Stanley

All governments lie and distort to advance their agendas. But it's fair to regard the current moment as a singular age of unreality in recent United States politics. Most members of one party have embraced an explicitly fictional world, one in which the 2020 election was stolen by rampant election fraud by Democrats. Historian Timothy Snyder has called this fabricated conspiracy "the Big Lie." The rise of such a flagrant mendacity is usually located very recently, in Donald Trump's first election run or in the dawning of the social media age. But the inflection point was actually 20 years ago, in the immediate aftermath of 9/11.

In *Mother Jones*, David Corn has argued that the George W. Bush administration paved the way for the Big Lie, on the grounds that its propaganda push that Iraq had weapons of mass destruction constituted its own "Big Lie." More generally, one might think that the misinformation-filled campaign in the lead-up to the Iraq War was itself an early example of the "post-truth" era. Admittedly, its effects on the promotion of false beliefs were extreme. We focus so much today on the role of social media and digital disinformation when it comes to our fractured sense of reality and the rise of conspiratorial thinking. But it's worth remembering that in September 2003–five months before a site called thefacebook.com went live–a *Washington Post* poll found that almost 70 percent of Americans thought that Saddam Hussein was at least somewhat likely to have been *personally* involved in the 9/11 attacks.

There is, however, a distinction between the distortions that the Bush-Cheney administration made in its rush to war and the "Big Lie" of Trump's Republican Party. As historian Joseph Stieb argued correctly in the *Washington Post*, unlike the Bush administration' propaganda, "Trump's case for a stolen election isn't exaggerated, it's pure fiction." In other words, the Bush administration attempted to deceive American citizens by distorting evidence and insinuating falsehoods. In intending to deceive, one treats one's audience as reasoners whom one must persuade. In contrast, Trump and the party he controls simply made up, whole cloth, a fictional reality for its own loyal audience. Trump's "Big Lie" was never intended to be digested by anyone other than unwavering supporters of the leader. A Big Lie isn't part of an argument. A Big Lie is a rallying cry.

How, then, did the immediate post-9/11 era give rise to our current politics? Some of the most trusted Americans in public life, such as Colin Powell, were used to present wildly exaggerated and false claims to the public. Much of the mainstream media felt impelled to give far more credibility to the government's justifications for the Iraq War than they warranted. When democratic institutions are revealed to have misled the public as badly as they did, what results in a crisis of legitimacy. In such a crisis, people look for a charismatic leader in whom they can place their faith. The failures of the Bush administration made Trump's takeover of the Republican Party possible, because the success of Trump's style of politics depends on a vast loss of public trust in government and the media.

It is not just the decline in public trust that paved the way for the flourishing of what can rightly be called fascist politics. After 9/11, Muslims were represented as an existential threat, domestically and internationally. Trump's favorite government institution, ICE, is a product of the post-9/11 era. The logic of a militarized border, with a massive department of "Homeland Security" and a designated internal police force to protect "us" against "them," is a legacy of that era. It's no wonder that social platforms have exploited the rise of this in-group versus out-group mentality, attuning their algorithms to profit off of powerful emotional triggers such as fear, outrage, and disgust.

Fascist politics thrives when democratic institutions can be painted as corrupt and untrustworthy. It thrives when a population is taught to fear a supposed enemy that is both foreign and yet insidiously domestic–be they Muslims, Jews (as in Nazi Germany) or another minority group. Social media and online influence operations provided platforms and fuel for conspiratorial thinking to proliferate. But it was the post-9/11 era, with its nativist anti-Muslim appeals, betrayals of public trust and failures of democratic institutions, that enabled a politics based on rallying cries and faith rather than mutual deliberation over policy. It laid the groundwork for the future success of politicians who prey on our fears and encourage conspiracy theories, if not manufacture them outright. This is how they push aside democracy in pursuit of absolute power.

About the Author

Jason Stanley is the Jacob Urowsky Professor of Philosophy at Yale University and the author of five books, most recently How Fascism Works.

Personality Type, as well as Politics, Predicts Who Shares Fake News

By Asher Lawson and Hemant Kakkar

Behavioral and political scientists have pointed fingers at political conservatives, as opposed to liberals, when it comes to spreading fake news stories. But not all conservatives do it, and sweeping generalizations threaten to condemn everyone who subscribes to conservative values. This approach risks even more dangerous polarization.

Political leanings are far from the only determinants of behavior. Personality is a crucial influence, so our research on misinformation sharing has focused on that. One widely used psychological system for identifying personality traits organizes them into five categories: openness to experience, conscientiousness, extroversion, agreeableness, and neuroticism. (It is called, unsurprisingly, the five-factor theory.) We looked specifically at conscientiousness, which captures differences in people's orderliness, impulse control, conventionality, and reliability.

In a series of eight studies with a total of 4,642 participants, we examined whether low-conscientiousness conservatives (LCCs) disseminate more misinformation than other conservatives or low-conscientiousness liberals. First we determined people's political ideology and conscientiousness through assessments that asked participants about their values and behaviors. We then showed the same people a series of real and fake news stories relating to COVID and asked them to rate how accurate the stories were. We also asked whether they would consider sharing each story.

Both liberals and conservatives sometimes saw false stories as accurate. This error was likely driven in part by their *wanting* certain stories to be true because they aligned with their beliefs.

But actually sharing false news was markedly higher among LCCs compared with everyone else in the study, although some people of all persuasions did it. There was no difference between liberals and conservatives with high levels of conscientiousness. Low-conscientiousness liberals did not share more misinformation than their high-conscientiousness liberal counterparts.

What explains the exceptional tendency of LCCs to share fake news? To explore this question, we gathered information about participants' politics and personalities and administered questionnaires to assess their need for chaos–the desire to disrupt and destroy the existing political and social institutions–as well as their support of conservative issues, support for Donald Trump, trust in mainstream media, and time spent on social media. LCCs, we learned, expressed a general desire for chaos, and this need may explain their proclivity to spread misinformation. Other factors, including support for Trump, were not as strongly related.

Unfortunately, our work on this personality trait also suggests that accuracy labels on news stories will not solve the problem of misinformation. We ran a study where we explicitly stated whether each news story in question was false, using a "disputed" tag commonly seen on social media, or true, using a "supported" tag. We found that the supported tag increased the rate at which real stories were shared among both liberals and conservatives. LCCs, however, continued to share misinformation at a greater rate despite the clear warnings that the stories were false.

We ran another study that involved explicitly telling participants that an article they wanted to share was inaccurate. People then had the chance to change their choice. Not only did LCCs still share fake news at a higher rate than others in the study, but they also were comparatively insensitive to direct warnings that the stories they wanted to share were false.

The poor effectiveness of warnings among LCCs is worrying because our research suggests these people are primary drivers of fake-news proliferation. Social media networks therefore need to find a different solution than just tagging stories with warning labels. Interventions based on the assumption that truth matters to readers may be inadequate. Another option might involve social media companies monitoring fake news that has the potential to hurt others, such as misinformation related to vaccines and elections, and actively removing such content from their platforms.

Whatever the case, until these companies find an approach that works, this problem will persist. In the interim, our society will pay the cost of spreading misinformation. The long, conspiratorial road that rioters followed to the January 2021 Capitol insurrection shows that this spread can have serious and damaging consequences.

About the Authors

Asher Lawson is a graduate student in Duke University's Management and Organizations program.

Hemant Kakkar is an assistant professor of management at Duke University's Fuqua School of Business.

Liberals and Conservatives Are Both Susceptible to Fake News, but for Different Reasons

By Scott Barry Kaufman

Humans are motivated reasoners. When we see a news article that confirms something we think to be true or we *want* to be true, we quickly "like" it and then share it vehemently on Facebook. Take a news story, for instance, which declares that "Cheese protects you from all causes of death, says science." Most cheese lovers probably didn't look too deeply into the scientific literature before they shared it among their friends.

This applies not just to scientific news stories but also to politically-based "fake news." Since the 2016 presidency, the use of the phrase exploded, with a more than 350% increase in popular usage. Collins Dictionary even named it word of the year in 2017. Surprisingly, however, the concept of fake news has received little attention within the social psychological literature. Is everyone susceptible to believing fake news, or is it mostly just Republicans (as anecdotes suggest)?

In a recent preprint, Craig Harper and Thom Baguley presented the results of three well-powered studies using American and British samples to investigate whether liberals and conservatives are equally motivated to believe fake news. The researchers presented both positive and negative fake news stories written for the purposes of the study. For each story, a 'TV breaking news' image was shown, along with a short written news story to supplement the image.

For instance, in the first study stories were either favorable or unfavorable about either former President Barack Obama or current President Donald Trump. Favorable stories reported that the target had donated $50 million of their personal fortune to selected charities, while the unfavorable stories reported that the target was facing criminal charges related to voter fraud in the

2016 Presidential election. Participants then made "legitimacy judgments" of each story, rating how much they believed the story to be true, reliable, and trustworthy. This is what they found.

Are Liberals and Conservatives Equally Susceptible to Fake News?

The answer is yes. The researchers found that people on both sides of the traditional left-right divide are equally likely to believe political news that is consistent with their ideology, and to disbelieve news that is inconsistent with their side. For instance, liberals judged the anti-Trump story as being much more legitimate than the pro-Trump story, with conservatives showing the opposite judgment.

Interestingly, these effects were even more pronounced when they replaced binary party preferences with party warmth judgments. In other words, if you are *way* left or *way* right you are even more likely to cognitively distort yourself in all sorts of ways to either believe the news (if it supports your party) or bend over backwards to disconfirm it (if it disconfirms your party's line). The researchers conclude that "people infer news legitimacy in a way that appears motivated by their own ideological positioning." These findings are very much in line with Jonathan Haidt's account of motivated reasoning being a big source of divisions in politics and religion.

This finding is also consistent with other research suggesting that there are symmetries among both liberals and conservatives when it comes to motivated reasoning. For instance, liberals and conservatives are similarly motivated to avoid exposure to one another's opinions, and are similarly motivated to deny scientific findings that are inconsistent with their ideology.

On the slightly more hopeful side, the average ratings of legitimacy of fake news for both groups was below the midpoint of the scale. This suggests that most people do have at least some capacity to discern true stories from those that are false. In fact, the researchers found it was important to consider three particular variables to determine whether someone within their party would be *particularly* susceptible to fake news.

Thinking Styles and Collective Narcissism

We each differ in our preferred mode of thinking. Some people tend to think with their head and are motivated to seek out and process information, whereas others tend to think with their gut, motivated to action by their instincts and intuitions. You may think that those who report that they are super rational and logical would be less likely to fall prey to motivated reasoning, right? Well, the results may surprise you.

The researchers measured individual differences in thinking styles and found that regardless of the political party identification, when high need for cognition individuals were presented with fake news stories that were consistent with their ideology, they were even *more* likely than everyone else to judge the story as legitimate, and when they were faced with fake news story that were inconsistent with their ideology, they were even less likely to consider the news legitimate than everyone else.

One possible explanation is that highly logical and rational people are not only more likely to disbelieve politically inconsistent news stories along tribal lines, but they are also more likely to seek out further disconfirming information, thus exaggerating their disbelief of politically inconsistent stories. This is consistent with research showing that people who score high in need for cognition tend to build information-rich social networks, but of course this can be problematic when your rich social networks are still operating in an echo chamber.

The researchers found some asymmetries, however. Conservatives who scored high in faith intuition (i.e., those who tend to think with their gut instincts) had higher perceptions of the legitimacy among fake news, although this variable had little effect on the judgments of liberals. The researchers suggest that conservatives may be most susceptible on average to fall prey to fake news stories, considering that they are the group most likely to be exposed to such material online, and they are also the group with the highest average levels of faith in intuition.

However, liberals aren't off the hook, as they are statistically more likely to use investment in the righteousness of their political viewpoints to believe politically consistent news stories and their higher level of need for cognition to delegitimize politically inconsistent news stories. The researchers found that liberals who scored higher in a measure of "collective narcissism"—which measures a tendency to invest in, and perceive superiority of, your political views–showed exaggerated legitimacy judgments for the politically consistent (e.g., anti-Trump) fake news stories. This data is interesting because it suggests that collective narcissism is not only a right-wing populist phenomenon.

Taken together, all of these findings are consistent with an identity-based approach to the understanding of politically and ideologically motivated engagement with "fake news." It's clear that we must view fake news engagement through a motivated reasoning lens and that both conservatives and liberals can fall prey to fake news, even though the underlying motives may differ within each group.

These findings further emphasize the importance of really thinking through how the spread of political misinformation at a societal level can impact the political landscape. As the researchers note, "it might not be enough to ask people to think more critically about political views. Instead, we might look to reduce the effects of online echo chambers and facilitate greater levels of communication between those with opposing political outlooks."

While social media has the potential to divide, we must not forget that it also has the potential to expose people to ideologically diverse viewpoints.

About the Author

Scott Barry Kaufman, Ph.D., is a humanistic psychologist exploring the depths of human potential. He has taught courses on intelligence, creativity, and well-being at Columbia University, NYU, the University of Pennsylvania, and elsewhere. He hosts The Psychology Podcast, and is author and/or editor of nine books, including Transcend: The New Science of Self-Actualization, Wired to Create: Unravelling the Mysteries of the Creative Mind *(with Carolyn Gregoire), and* Ungifted: Intelligence Redefined. *In 2015, he was named one of "50 Groundbreaking Scientists who are changing the way we see the world" by* Business Insider. *He wrote the extremely popular* Beautiful Minds *blog for* Scientific American *for close to a decade.*

Fake News Websites May Not Have a Major Effect on Elections

By Karen Weintraub

During the 2016 election cycle, certain websites spread false information across the Internet. But a new study suggests they did not have as much impact as some have feared.

About 44 percent of voters, mostly right-leaning, saw at least one site, the study found. Yet those voters also saw plenty of legitimate news online. "This content, while worrisome, is only a small fraction of most people's information," says Brendan Nyhan, a professor of government at Dartmouth College and one of the three authors of the study, which was published in March 2020 in *Nature Human Behaviour*.

The research provided the most systematic examination of people's exposure to these fringe websites to date. It showed that while these untrustworthy sources might have a small effect on public opinion, in 2016 they did not substantially move individuals' positions about then presidential candidate Donald Trump or whether to go to the polls.

Emily Thorson, an assistant professor of political science at Syracuse University, says she is not surprised that these sites did not have a huge effect. A single piece of information rarely changes anyone's opinion, "whether it's true–or false," says Thorson, who was not involved in the new study. "That's a good thing." The idea that a handful of unreliable outlets were going to substantially alter views or behaviors "is pretty far-fetched, given what we know about the stability of people's political attitudes," she says.

The research paired responses to an online survey with data about which websites participants visited. In 2016 the survey responses were collected from 3,251 volunteers between October 21 and 31, and the web traffic was recorded between October 7 and November 14. The election was held that year on November 8.

The study "is consistent with, and adds to, prior research that suggests that while a fair number of people had some exposure to 'fake news,' that the exposure was highly concentrated among a small number of conservatives," says David Lazer, University Distinguished Professor of political science and computer and information science at Northeastern University.

Lazer, who provided feedback for the paper but was not involved in the work, notes that it examined an individual's browsing behavior, whereas previous studies looked solely at sharing false information on Facebook or, in the case of his own research, on exposure to, and dissemination of, such content on Twitter.

In his study, Lazer and his colleagues showed that untrue material accounted for nearly 6 percent of all news consumed on the Twitter. But only 1 percent of users were exposed to 80 percent of this misinformation, and 0.1 percent shared 80 percent of it.

Nyhan and his colleagues' new research concludes that most people find these untrustworthy websites through social media, particularly Facebook. "It shows Facebook as a major conduit to fake news [and] misinformation," Lazer says.

Thorson says that while the *Nature Human Behaviour* study was expensive and difficult to conduct, Facebook already has much of the same information readily available–and should provide more of it to researchers. "One of the big takeaways for me is how important it is to start being able to look inside of what Facebook is doing," she says.

In 2018 voters were less exposed to misleading content than they had been in 2016, Nyhan says. But it is unclear if that reduction is because social media platforms such as Facebook were taking measures to minimize the effects of these fringe sites or whether there was simply less activity during a midterm election year.

Nyhan adds that he and his colleagues conducted the study because of shortcomings they saw in some other research and common misconceptions about the role of these websites. "I do worry that people's often incorrect sense of the prevalence of this type of content is leading them to support more extreme responses," he says.

Measures to halt the transmission of material can "raise important concerns about the free flow of information and the exercise of power by the platforms over the information that people see."

The main problem with these sites, Nyhan says, is not what they post but the risk that someone in power will amplify their lies. "One implication of our study is that most of the misinformation that people get about politics doesn't come from these fringe websites. It comes from the mainstream–it comes from the media and political figures who are the primary sources of political news and commentary," he says.

A website might promote unscientific theories about the origins of the coronavirus without changing a lot of minds, Nyhan says. But when someone like conservative commentator Rush Limbaugh talks on air about those same theories, it has a bigger effect, he adds.

Will the 2020 election prove to be any different than the one in 2016 in terms of the power of these fringe sites? It is too soon to tell, Nyhan says. "The public is at least potentially more aware of the issue, though I don't know of any systematic evidence helping them make better choices," he says. The year "2020 will be the first real test."

About the Author

Karen Weintraub is a staff writer at USA Today, *where she covers COVID, vaccine development and other health issues. She is the coauthor with Michael Kuchta of* Born In Cambridge: 400 Years of Ideas and Innovators *(The MIT Press, 2022).*

Russian Misinformation Seeks to Confound, Not Convince

By David Robert Grimes

As war envelops Ukraine, Russian sources have strived to create a miasma of disinformation about the invasion. Among ample efforts to distort reality, the Russian Ministry of Defense asserted recently that U.S.-backed labs in Ukraine have been developing bioweapons. Outlandish as this falsehood may be, Fox's Tucker Carlson gave it credence by arguing that the U.S. government's response was a "cover-up."

As the Russia-Ukraine war intensifies, so too will the flow of disinformation. This is an age-old strategy Russia has long history of employing, and a playbook that others, most notably anti-vaccine activists, have borrowed from liberally. Yet, rather than focusing effort on convincing people of a falsehood, the Russian strategy takes a tack reminiscent of a strategy long employed by the tobacco industry: to sow so much doubt about what is true that it sends people into decision paralysis. Faced with a cacophony of wild and conflicting claims, people do nothing, unsure of what is right.

Despite constituting only a small part of our media diet, disinformation campaigns, in our digital world, can be devastatingly effective. We are intrinsically biased towards information that is emotionally visceral. We afford more weight to content that frightens or outrages us, with the ability to induce anger serving as the single greatest predictor of whether content goes viral. This propels the most visceral, divisive narratives to the forefront of discourse, creating a sound and fury of passionately debated claims and counter claims. In that atmosphere, it becomes increasingly difficult to ascertain what to believe and easy to abandon the task of discerning the truth.

If we are not to fall victim to such rank dishonesty, it is crucial now that we question our sources more carefully than ever before.

Indecision and distraction have long been central to Russia's *dezinformatsiya* (disinformation) policy, a term Stalin himself is credited with coining. While an ancient concept, Russia had by the imperial age mastered dark obfuscation techniques refined for the era of mass communication. By the dawn of the Soviet empire, they realized this potential on an industrial scale, establishing the world's first office dedicated to disinformation in 1923. In the 1960s, the KGB covertly sponsored American fringe groups, amplifying conspiratorial narratives about everything from the assassination of president John F. Kennedy to water fluoridation.

The goal, as KGB Major General Oleg Kalugin elucidated in 1998, was "not intelligence collection, but subversion: active measures to weaken the West, to drive wedges in the Western community alliances of all sorts, particularly NATO, to sow discord among allies, to weaken the United States in the eyes of the people of Europe, Asia, Africa, Latin America....". Operation INFEKTION, a mid-1980s clandestine effort to spread the myth that AIDS was a CIA-designed bioweapon, was but one infamous exemplar. While utterly fictitious, it resonated with communities ravaged by HIV and neglected by the callous indifference of the Reagan administration. Despite Russian intelligence taking responsibility for this lie in 1992, the legacy of AIDS denialism persists to this day worldwide.

During the Cold War, the doctrine of "active measures" was the beating heart of Soviet intelligence. This philosophy of political and information warfare had wide remit, including front groups, media manipulation, counterfeiting, infiltrating peace groups, and even committing the occasional assassination.

And in our media-saturated era, Russia has been, by far, disinformation's most enthusiastic user. Take the 2016 U.S. presidential election and the contentious Brexit referendum; Russia appears to have influenced both via lies and distortions.

But disinformation is not solely confined to geopolitics. By summer 2020, the European Commission identified a concerted Russian drive to propagate COVID disinformation worldwide. From the outset of the pandemic, Kremlin-backed troll farms pushed the narrative that COVID was an engineered bioweapon, peddling the explosive fiction that 5G radio frequencies caused the virus–a lie that resulted in dozens of arson attacks on cell towers worldwide.

There is a dark irony in the observation that conspiracy-minded people can be weaponized in plots to which they're entirely oblivious. The enduring popularity of the virus-as-a-bioweapon mantra is a stark reminder that in the age of social media, such manipulation has become ever easier and more effective. Perhaps the most odious example of this is the cynical rise of anti-vaccine propaganda.

The sheer efficacy of vaccination is scientifically incontrovertible, and after clean water, immunization is the most life-saving intervention in human history. Despite this, the last decade has witnessed precipitous drops in vaccine confidence worldwide. The renaissance of once virtually conquered diseases prompted the WHO to declare vaccine hesitancy a top-10 threat to public health in 2019.

Vaccine hesitancy is a spectrum rather than a simple binary, and exposure to anti-vaccine conspiracy theories nudges recipients towards rejection. But critically, many who decline vaccination are not dyed-in-the-wool anti-vaccine zealots, but simply scared by what they have heard, unsure what to believe. Our tendency towards the illusory truth effect exacerbates this inertia, as the mere repetition of a fiction is enough to prime us to accept it, even if we know it to be false on an intellectual level. While Russia has often amplified anti-vaccine conspiracy theories to increase tensions, the anti-vaccine movements exist independently of these efforts, and are masters at sowing the seeds of doubt with torrents of conflicting and emotive claims.

This illustrates the grim reality that disinformation has no need for consistency and zero commitment to objective reality; claims are frequently contradictory, arguing both sides of the coin in exaggerated and divisive ways. This "Russian firehose" model of propaganda is high-output, contradictory, and multichannel. The stream encourages us to sleepwalk into apathy, distrustful of everything. This renders us supremely malleable, and dangerously disengaged.

When it comes to vaccination, concerned parents often opt to stay with the devil they know, delaying or even rejecting vaccination rather than sifting through the symphony of conflicting claims to which they're subjected. Similarly, the outpouring of fictions about Ukraine, its president, Volodymyr Zelensky, and the war is designed to overwhelm our capacity to analyze, inducing us to implicitly accept uncertainty over aggressor and aggrieved–a manufactured doubt benefiting Russia and other nations.

Conviction is not the chief goal of disinformation; instilling doubt is. This is why anti-vaccine activists have been so successful online, and why Russian troll-farms push ample resources into hawking lies virtually everywhere. The ubiquity of these fictions gives them an implicit veneer of legitimacy, fueling polarization and distrust.

This is the strategy Putin continues to pursue; already Russian propaganda has tried to paint Ukraine (or NATO / America) as aggressors with staged disinformation. This has been rendered less effective by the Biden administration's creative approach of releasing intelligence prior to the operation. Across social media, Russian front organizations still try to induce doubt, efforts that will only intensify as the war wages on. Truth, the old adage insists, is the first casualty of war.

About the Author

David Robert Grimes is a scientist and author of Good Thinking: Why Flawed Logic Puts Us All at Risk and How Critical Thinking Can Save the World *(The Experiment). His work focuses on health disinformation and conspiracy theory, and he is an international advocate for the public understanding of science. He is a recipient of the Nature/Sense about Science Maddox Prize, and a fellow of the Committee for Skeptical Inquiry.*

Clicks, Lies and Videotape

By Brooke Borel

In April 2018 a new video of Barack Obama surfaced on the Internet. Against a backdrop that included both the American and presidential flags, it looked like many of his previous speeches. Wearing a crisp white shirt and dark suit, Obama faced the camera and punctuated his words with outstretched hands: "President Trump is a total and complete dipshit."

Without cracking a smile, he continued. "Now, you see, I would never say these things. At least not in a public address. But someone else would." The view shifted to a split screen, revealing the actor Jordan Peele. Obama hadn't said anything–it was a real recording of an Obama address blended with Peele's impersonation. Side by side, the message continued as Peele, like a digital ventriloquist, put more words in the former president's mouth.

In this era of fake news, the video was a public service announcement produced by *BuzzFeed News*, showcasing an application of new artificial-intelligence (AI) technology that could do for audio and video what Photoshop has done for digital images: allow for the manipulation of reality.

The results are still fairly unsophisticated. Listen and watch closely, and Obama's voice is a bit nasally. For brief flashes, his mouth–fused with Peele's–floats off-center. But this rapidly evolving technology, which is intended for Hollywood film editors and video game makers, has the imaginations of some national security experts and media scholars running dark. The next generation of these tools may make it possible to create convincing fakes from scratch–not by warping existing footage, as in the Obama address, but by orchestrating scenarios that never happened at all.

The consequences for public knowledge and discourse could be profound. Imagine, for instance, the impact on the upcoming elections if a fake video smeared a politician during a tight race. Or attacked a CEO the night before a public offering. A group could stage a terrorist attack and fool news outlets into covering it, sparking knee-jerk retribution. Even if a viral video is later proved to be fake, will the public still believe it was true anyway? And perhaps most troubling: What if the very idea of pervasive fakes makes us stop believing much of what we see and hear—including the stuff that is real?

Many technologists acknowledge the potential for sweeping misuse of this technology. But while they fixate on "sexy solutions for detection and disclosure, they spend very little time figuring out whether any of that actually has an effect on people's beliefs on the validity of fake video," says Nate Persily, a law professor at Stanford University. Persily studies, among other topics, how the Internet affects democracy, and he is among a growing group of researchers who argue that curbing viral disinformation cannot be done through technical fixes alone. It will require input from psychologists, social scientists, and media experts to help tease out how the technology will land in the real world.

"We've got to do this now," Persily says, "because at the moment the technologists—necessarily—drive the discussion" on what may be possible with AI-generated video. Already our trust in democratic institutions such as government and journalism is ebbing. With social media a dominant distribution channel for information, it is even easier today for fake-news makers to exploit us. And with no cohesive strategy in place to confront an increasingly sophisticated technology, our fragile collective trust is even more at risk.

Innocuous Beginnings

The path to fake video traces back to the 1960s, when computer-generated imagery was first conceived. In the 1980s these special effects went mainstream, and ever since, movie lovers have watched the technology evolve from science-fiction flicks to Forrest Gump shaking hands with John F. Kennedy in 1994 to the revival of Peter Cushing and Carrie Fisher in *Rogue One*. The goal has always been to "create a digital world where any storytelling could be possible," says

Hao Li, an associate professor of computer science at the University of Southern California and CEO of Pinscreen, an augmented-reality start-up. "How can we create something that appears real, but everything is actually virtual?"

Early on, most graphics came from artists, who used computers to create three-dimensional models and then hand-painted textures and other details–a tedious process that did not scale up. About 20 years ago some computer-vision researchers started thinking of graphics differently: rather than spending time on individual models, why not teach computers to create from data? In 1997 scientists at the Interval Research Corporation in Palo Alto, Calif., developed Video Rewrite, which sliced up existing footage and reconfigured it. The researchers made a clip of JFK saying, "I never met Forrest Gump." Soon after, scientists at the Max Planck Institute for Biological Cybernetics in Tübingen, Germany, taught a computer to pull features from a data set of 200 three-dimensional scans of human faces to make a new face.

The biggest recent jump in the relationship among computer vision, data, and automation arguably came in 2012, with advances in a type of AI called deep learning. Unlike the work from the late 1990s, which used static data and never improved, deep learning adapts and gets better. This technique reduces objects, such as a face, to bits of data, says Xiaochang Li, now in the department of communication at Stanford. "This is the moment where engineers say: we are no longer going to model things," she says. "We are going to model our ignorance of things and just run the data to understand patterns."

Deep learning uses layers of simple mathematical formulas called neural networks, which get better at a task over time. For example, computer scientists can teach a deep-learning tool to recognize human faces by feeding it hundreds or thousands of photographs and essentially saying, each time, this is a face or this is not a face. Eventually when the tool encounters a new person, it will recognize patterns that make up human features and say, statistically speaking, this is also a face.

Next came the ability to concoct faces that looked like real people, using deep-learning tools known as generative networks. The same logic applies: computer scientists train the networks on hundreds or thousands of images. But this time the network follows the patterns it gleaned from the examples to make a new face. Some companies are now using the same approach with audio. In 2018, Google unveiled Duplex, an AI assistant based on software called WaveNet, which can make phone calls and sounds like a real person—complete with verbal tics such as uhs and hmms. In the future, a fake video of a politician may not need to rely on impersonations from actors like Peele. In April 2017 Lyrebird, a Canadian start-up, released sample audio that sounded creepily like Obama, Trump, and Hillary Clinton.

But generative networks need big data sets for training, and that can require significant human labor. The next step in improving virtual content was to teach the AI to train itself. In 2014 researchers at the University of Montreal did this with a generative adversarial network, or GAN, which puts two neural networks in conversation. The first is a generator, which makes fake images, and the second is a discriminator, which learns to distinguish between real and fake. With little to no human supervision, the networks train one another through competition—the discriminator nudges the generator to make increasingly realistic fakes, while the generator keeps trying to trick the discriminator. GANs can craft all sorts of stuff. At the University of California, Berkeley, scientists built one that can turn images of horses into zebras or transform Impressionist paintings by the likes of Monet into crisp, photorealistic scenes.

Then, in May 2018, researchers at the Max Planck Institute for Informatics in Saarbrücken, Germany, and their colleagues revealed "deep video," which uses a type of GAN. It allows an actor to control the mouth, eyes and facial movements of someone else in prerecorded footage. Deep video currently only works in a portrait setup, where a person looks directly at the camera. If the actor moves too much, the resulting video has noticeable digital artifacts such as blurred pixels around the face.

GANs are not yet capable of building complex scenes in video that are indistinguishable from ones captured in real footage. Sometimes GANs produce oddities, such as a person with an eyeball growing out of his or her forehead. In February 2018, however, researchers at the company NVIDIA figured out a way to get GANs to make incredibly high-resolution faces by starting the training on relatively small photographs and then building up the resolution step by step. And Hao Li's team at the University of Southern California has used GANs to make realistic skin, teeth and mouths, all of which are notoriously difficult to digitally reconstruct.

None of these technologies are easy for nonexperts to use well. But BuzzFeed's experiment hints at our possible future. The video came from free software called FakeApp—which used deep learning, though not GAN. The resulting videos are dubbed deepfakes, a mash-up of "deep learning" and "fake," named after a user on the website Reddit, who, along with others, was an early adopter and used the tech to swap celebrities' faces into porn. Since then, amateurs across the Web have used FakeApp to make countless videos—most of them relatively harmless pranks, such as adding actor Nicolas Cage to a bunch of movies he was not in or morphing Trump's face onto the body of German chancellor Angela Merkel. More ominous are the implications. Now that the technology is democratized, anyone with a computer can hypothetically use it.

Conditions for Fake News

Experts have long worried that computer-enabled editing would ruin reality. Back in 2000, an article in *MIT Technology Review* about products such as Video Rewrite warned that "seeing is no longer believing" and that an image "on the evening news could well be a fake—a fabrication of fast new video-manipulation technology." Twenty years later fake videos don't seem to be flooding news shows. For one thing, it is still hard to produce a really good one. It took 56 hours for *BuzzFeed* to make the Obama clip with help from a professional video editor.

The way we consume information, however, has changed. Today only about half of American adults watch the news on television, whereas two-thirds get at least some news via social media, according to the Pew Research Center. The Internet has allowed for a proliferation of media outlets that cater to niche audiences–including hyperpartisan websites that intentionally stoke anger, unimpeded by traditional journalistic standards. The Internet rewards viral content that we are able to share faster than ever before, Persily says. And the glitches in fake video are less discernible on a tiny mobile screen than a living-room TV.

The question now is what will happen if a deepfake with significant social or political implications goes viral. With such a new, barely studied frontier, the short answer is that we do not know, says Julie Carpenter, a research fellow with the Ethics + Emerging Sciences Group, based at California State Polytechnic University, San Luis Obispo, who studies human-robot interaction. It is possible we will find out soon enough, with key elections coming up this fall in the U.S., as well as internationally.

We have already witnessed the fallout when connectivity and disinformation collide. Fake news–fabricated text stories designed to look like legitimate news reports and to go viral–was a much discussed feature of the 2016 U.S. presidential election. According to collaborative research from Princeton University, Dartmouth College, and the University of Exeter in England, roughly one in four Americans visited a fake news site during the five weeks between October 7 and November 14, 2016, mostly through the conduit of their Facebook feeds. Moreover, 2016 marked a low point in the public's trust in journalism. By one estimate, just 51 percent of Democrats and 14 percent of Republicans said they trusted mass media.

The science on written fake news is limited. But some research suggests that seeing false information just once is sufficient to make it seem plausible later on, says Gordon Pennycook, an assistant professor of organizational behavior at the University of Regina in Saskatchewan. It is not clear why, but it may be thanks to "fluency," he says, or "the ease at which it is processed." If we hear Obama call Trump a curse word and then later encounter another false instance where Obama calls Trump obscene names, we may be primed to think it is real because it is familiar.

According to a study from the Massachusetts Institute of Technology that tracked 126,000 stories on Twitter between 2006 and 2017, we are also more likely to share fake news than real news–and especially fake political stories, which spread further and quicker than those about money, natural disasters or terrorism. The paper suggested that people crave novelty. Fake news in general plays to our emotions and personal identity, enticing us to react before we have had a chance to process the information and decide if it is worth spreading. The more that content surprises, scares, or enrages us, the more we seem to share it.

There are troubling clues that video may be especially effective at stoking fear. "When you process information visually, you believe that this thing is closer to you in terms of space, time or social group," says Elinor Amit, an assistant professor of cognitive, linguistic and psychological sciences at Brown University, whose work teases out the differences in how we relate to text and images. She hypothesizes that this distinction is evolutionary–our visual development came before written language, and we rely more on our senses to detect immediate danger.

Fake video has, in fact, already struck political campaigns. In July 2018 Allie Beth Stuckey, a TV host at Conservative Review, posted on Facebook an interview with Alexandria Ocasio-Cortez, a Democratic congressional nominee from New York City. The video was not a deepfake but an old-fashioned splice of a real interview with new questions to make Ocasio-Cortez appear to flub her answers. Depending on your political persuasion, the video was either a smear job or, as Stuckey later called it in her defense, satire. Either way, it had 3.4 million views within a week and more than 5,000 comments. Some viewers seemed to think Ocasio-Cortez had bombed a real interview. "Omg! She doesn't know what and how to answer," one wrote. "She is stupid."

That all of this is worrying is part of the problem. Our dark ruminations may actually be worse for society than the videos themselves. Politicians could sow doubt when their real misdeeds are caught on tape by claiming they were faked, for example. Knowing that convincing fakes are even possible might erode our trust in all media, says Raymond J. Pingree, an associate professor in mass communications at Louisiana State University. Pingree studies how confident people are in their ability to evaluate what is real and what is not and how that affects their willingness to participate in the political process. When individuals lose that confidence, they are more likely to fall for liars and crooks, he says, and "it can make people stop wanting to seek the truth."

A Game of Cat and Mouse

To a computer scientist, the solution to a bug is often just more computer science. Although the bugs in question here are far more complex than bad coding, there is a sense in the community that algorithms could be built to flag the fakes.

"There is certainly technical progress that can be made against the problem," says R. David Edelman of M.I.T.'s Internet Policy Research Initiative. Edelman, who served as a tech adviser under Obama, has been impressed by faked videos of the former president. "I know the guy. I wrote speeches for him. I couldn't tell the difference between the real and fake video," he says. But while he could be fooled, Edelman says, an algorithm might pick up on the "telltale tics and digital signatures" that are invisible to the human eye.

So far the fixes fall within two categories. One proves that a video is real by embedding digital signatures, analogous to the intricate seals, holograms and other features that currency printers use to thwart counterfeiters. Every digital camera would have a unique signature, which, theoretically, would be tough to copy.

The second strategy is to automatically flag fake videos with detectors. Arguably the most significant push for such a detector is a program from the Defense Advanced Research Projects Agency called Media Forensics, or MediFor. It kicked off in 2015, not long after a Russian news channel aired fake satellite images of a Ukrainian fighter jet shooting at Malaysia Airlines Flight 17. Later, a team of international investigators pegged the flight's downing on a Russian missile. The satellite images were not made with deep learning, but DARPA saw the coming revolution and wanted to find a way to fight it, says David Doermann, MediFor's former program manager.

MediFor is taking three broad approaches, which can be automated with deep learning. The first examines a video's digital fingerprint for anomalies. The second ensures a video follows the laws of physics, such as sunlight falling the way it would in the real world. And the third checks for external data, such as the weather on the day it was allegedly filmed. DARPA plans to unify these detectors into a single tool, which will give a point score on the likelihood that a video is fake.

These strategies could cut down on the volume of fakes, but it will still be a game of cat and mouse, with forgers imitating digital watermarks or building deep-learning tools to trick the detectors. "We will not win this game," says Alexei Efros, a professor of computer science and electrical engineering at U.C. Berkeley, who is collaborating with MediFor. "It's just that we will make it harder and harder for the bad guys to play it."

And anyway, these tools are still decades away, says Hany Farid, a professor of computer science at Dartmouth College. As fake video continues to improve, the only existing technical solution is to rely on digital forensics experts like Farid. "There's just literally a handful of people in the world you can talk to about this," he says. "I'm one of them. I don't scale to the Internet."

Saving Reality

Even if each of us can ultimately use detectors to parse the Internet, there will always be a lag between lies and truth. That is one reason why halting the spread of fake video is a challenge for the social media industry. "This is as much a distribution problem as it is a creation problem," Edelman says. "If a deepfake falls in the forest, no one hears it unless Twitter and Facebook amplify it."

When it comes to curbing viral disinformation, it is not clear what the legal obligations are for social media companies or whether the industry can be regulated without trampling free speech. Facebook CEO Mark Zuckerberg finally admitted that his platform has played a role in spreading fake news–although it took more than 10 months following the 2016 election. Facebook, after all, was designed to keep users consuming and spreading content, prioritizing what is popular over what is true. With more than two billion active monthly users, it is a tinderbox for anyone who wants to spark an enraging fake story.

Since then, Zuckerberg has promised to act. He is putting some of the burden on users by asking them to rank the trustworthiness of news sources (a move that some see as shirking responsibility) and plans to use AI to flag disinformation. The company has been tight-lipped on the details. Some computer scientists are skeptical about the AI angle, including Farid, who says the promises are "spectacularly naïve." Few independent scientists have been able to study how fake news spreads on Facebook because much of the relevant data has been on lockdown.

Still, all the algorithms and data in the world will not save us from disinformation campaigns if the researchers building fake-video technology do not grapple with how their products will be used and abused after they leave the lab. "This is my plea," Persily says, "that the hard scientists who do this work have to be paired up with the psychologists and the political scientists and the communication specialists–who have been working on these issues for a while." That kind of collaboration has been rare.

In March 2018, however, the Finnish Center for Artificial Intelligence announced a program that will invite psychologists, philosophers, ethicists and others to help AI researchers to grasp the broader social implications of their work. A month later Persily, along with Gary King, a political scientist at Harvard University, launched the Social Data Initiative. The project will, for the first time, allow social scientists to access Facebook data to study the spread of disinformation.

With a responsibility vacuum at the top, the onus of rooting out fake videos is falling on journalists and citizen sleuths. Near the end of the deepfake video of Obama and Peele, both men say: "Moving forward, we need to be more vigilant with what we trust from the Internet. It's a time when we need to rely on trusted news sources." It may have been a fake, but it was true.

About the Author

Brooke Borel is a journalist and author of The Chicago Guide to Fact-Checking. *She recently competed against an AI fact-checker and won by a worrying margin.*

Section 5: Improving Media Literacy

5.1 Misinformation Has Created a New World Disorder
By Claire Wardle

5.2 Schoolkids Are Falling Victim to Disinformation and Conspiracy Fantasies
By Melinda Wenner Moyer

5.3 We Should Teach Media Literacy in Elementary School
By Prateek Puri

5.4 The Psychology of Fact-Checking
By Stephen J. Ceci and Wendy M. Williams

5.5 (Dis)trust in Science
By Gleb Tsipursky

Misinformation Has Created a New World Disorder

By Claire Wardle

As someone who studies the impact of misinformation on society, I often wish the young entrepreneurs of Silicon Valley who enabled communication at speed had been forced to run a 9/11 scenario with their technologies before they deployed them commercially.

One of the most iconic images from that day shows a large clustering of New Yorkers staring upward. The power of the photograph is that we know the horror they're witnessing. It is easy to imagine that, today, almost everyone in that scene would be holding a smartphone. Some would be filming their observations and posting them to Twitter and Facebook. Powered by social media, rumors, and misinformation would be rampant. Hate-filled posts aimed at the Muslim community would proliferate, the speculation and outrage boosted by algorithms responding to unprecedented levels of shares, comments, and likes. Foreign agents of disinformation would amplify the division, driving wedges between communities and sowing chaos. Meanwhile those stranded on the tops of the towers would be livestreaming their final moments.

Stress testing technology in the context of the worst moments in history might have illuminated what social scientists and propagandists have long known: that humans are wired to respond to emotional triggers and share misinformation if it reinforces existing beliefs and prejudices. Instead designers of the social platforms fervently believed that connection would drive tolerance and counteract hate. They failed to see how technology would not change who we are fundamentally–it could only map onto existing human characteristics.

Online misinformation has been around since the mid-1990s. But in 2016 several events made it broadly clear that darker forces had emerged: automation, microtargeting, and coordination were fueling information campaigns designed to manipulate public opinion at scale. Journalists in the Philippines started raising flags as Rodrigo Duterte rose to power, buoyed by intensive Facebook activity. This was followed by unexpected results in the Brexit referendum in June and then the U.S. presidential election in November–all of which sparked researchers to systematically investigate the ways in which information was being used as a weapon.

During the past four years the discussion around the causes of our polluted information ecosystem has focused almost entirely on actions taken (or not taken) by the technology companies. But this fixation is too simplistic. A complex web of societal shifts is making people more susceptible to misinformation and conspiracy. Trust in institutions is falling because of political and economic upheaval, most notably through ever widening income inequality. The effects of climate change are becoming more pronounced. Global migration trends spark concern that communities will change irrevocably. The rise of automation makes people fear for their jobs and their privacy.

Bad actors who want to deepen existing tensions understand these societal trends, designing content that they hope will so anger or excite targeted users that the audience will become the messenger. The goal is that users will use their own social capital to reinforce and give credibility to that original message.

Most of this content is designed not to persuade people in any particular direction but to cause confusion, to overwhelm and to undermine trust in democratic institutions from the electoral system to journalism. And although much is being made about preparing the U.S. electorate for the 2020 election, misleading and conspiratorial content did not begin with the 2016 presidential race, and it will not end after this one. As tools designed to manipulate and amplify content become cheaper and more accessible, it will be even easier to weaponize users as unwitting agents of disinformation.

Weaponizing Context

Generally, the language used to discuss the misinformation problem is too simplistic. Effective research and interventions require clear definitions, yet many people use the problematic phrase "fake news." Used by politicians around the world to attack a free press, the term is dangerous. Recent research shows that audiences increasingly connect it with the mainstream media. It is often used as a catchall to describe things that are not the same, including lies, rumors, hoaxes, misinformation, conspiracies, and propaganda, but it also papers over nuance and complexity. Much of this content does not even masquerade as news–it appears as memes, videos, and social posts on Facebook and Instagram.

In February 2017 I created seven types of "information disorder" in an attempt to emphasize the spectrum of content being used to pollute the information ecosystem. They included, among others, satire, which is not intended to cause harm but still has the potential to fool; fabricated content, which is 100 percent false and designed to deceive and do harm; and false context, which is when genuine content is shared with false contextual information. Later that year, technology journalist Hossein Derakhshan and I published a report that mapped out the differentiations among disinformation, misinformation, and malinformation.

Purveyors of *dis*information–content that is intentionally false and designed to cause harm–are motivated by three distinct goals: to make money; to have political influence, either foreign or domestic; and to cause trouble for the sake of it.

Those who spread *mis*information–false content shared by a person who does not realize it is false or misleading–are driven by sociopsychological factors. People are performing their identities on social platforms to feel connected to others, whether the "others" are a political party, parents who do not vaccinate their children, activists who are concerned about climate change, or those who belong to a certain religion, race, or ethnic group. Crucially, disinformation can turn into misinformation when people share disinformation without realizing it is false.

We added the term "*mal*information" to describe genuine information that is shared with an intent to cause harm. An example of this is when Russian agents hacked into emails from the

Democratic National Committee and the Hillary Clinton campaign and leaked certain details to the public to damage reputations.

Having monitored misinformation in eight elections around the world since 2016, I have observed a shift in tactics and techniques. The most effective disinformation has always been that which has a kernel of truth to it, and indeed most of the content being disseminated now is not fake–it is misleading. Instead of wholly fabricated stories, influence agents are reframing genuine content and using hyperbolic headlines. The strategy involves connecting genuine content with polarizing topics or people. Because bad actors are always one step (or many steps) ahead of platform moderation, they are relabeling emotive disinformation as satire so that it will not get picked up by fact-checking processes. In these efforts, context, rather than content, is being weaponized. The result is intentional chaos.

Take, for example, the edited video of House Speaker Nancy Pelosi that circulated in May 2019. It was a genuine video, but an agent of disinformation slowed down the video and then posted that clip to make it seem that Pelosi was slurring her words. Just as intended, some viewers immediately began speculating that Pelosi was drunk, and the video spread on social media. Then the mainstream media picked it up, which undoubtedly made many more people aware of the video than would have originally encountered it.

Research has found that traditionally reporting on misleading content can potentially cause more harm. Our brains are wired to rely on heuristics, or mental shortcuts, to help us judge credibility. As a result, repetition and familiarity are two of the most effective mechanisms for ingraining misleading narratives, even when viewers have received contextual information explaining why they should know a narrative is not true.

Bad actors know this: In 2018, media scholar Whitney Phillips published a report for the Data & Society Research Institute that explores how those attempting to push false and misleading narratives use techniques to encourage reporters to cover their narratives. Yet another recent report from the Institute for the Future found that only 15 percent of U.S. journalists had been trained in how to report on misinformation more responsibly. A central challenge now for reporters and fact checkers—and anyone with substantial reach, such as politicians and influencers—is how to untangle and debunk falsehoods such as the Pelosi video without giving the initial piece of content more oxygen.

Memes: A Misinformation Powerhouse

In January 2017 the NPR radio show *This American Life* interviewed a handful of Trump supporters at one of his inaugural events called the DeploraBall. These people had been heavily involved in using social media to advocate for the president. Of Trump's surprising ascendance, one of the interviewees explained: "We memed him into power.... We directed the culture."

The word "meme" was first used by theorist Richard Dawkins in his 1976 book, *The Selfish Gene*, to describe "a unit of cultural transmission or a unit of imitation," an idea, behavior or style that spreads quickly throughout a culture. During the past several decades the word has been appropriated to describe a type of online content that is usually visual and takes on a particular aesthetic design, combining colorful, striking images with block text. It often refers to other cultural and media events, sometimes explicitly but mostly implicitly.

This characteristic of implicit logic—a nod and wink to shared knowledge about an event or person—is what makes memes impactful. Enthymemes are rhetorical devices where the argument is made through the absence of the premise or conclusion. Often key references (a recent news event, a statement by a political figure, an advertising campaign, or a wider cultural trend) are not spelled out, forcing the viewer to connect the dots. This extra work required of the viewer is a persuasive technique because it pulls an individual into the feeling of being connected to others. If the meme is poking fun or invoking outrage at the expense of another group, those associations are reinforced even further.

The seemingly playful nature of these visual formats means that memes have not been acknowledged by much of the research and policy community as influential vehicles for disinformation, conspiracy, or hate. Yet the most effective misinformation is that which will be shared, and memes tend to be much more shareable than text. The entire narrative is visible in your feed; there is no need to click on a link. A 2019 book by An Xiao Mina, *Memes to Movements*, outlines how memes are changing social protests and power dynamics, but this type of serious examination is relatively rare.

Indeed, of the Russian-created posts and ads on Facebook related to the 2016 election, many were memes. They focused on polarizing candidates such as Bernie Sanders, Hillary Clinton, or Donald Trump and on polarizing policies such as gun rights and immigration. Russian efforts often targeted groups based on race or religion, such as Black Lives Matter or evangelical Christians. When the Facebook archive of Russian-generated memes was released, some of the commentary at the time centered on the lack of sophistication of the memes and their impact. But research has shown that when people are fearful, oversimplified narratives, conspiratorial explanation, and messages that demonize others become far more effective. These memes did just enough to drive people to click the share button.

Technology platforms such as Facebook, Instagram, Twitter, and Pinterest play a significant role in encouraging this human behavior because they are designed to be performative in nature. Slowing down to check whether content is true before sharing it is far less compelling than reinforcing to your "audience" on these platforms that you love or hate a certain policy. The business model for so many of these platforms is attached to this identity performance because it encourages you to spend more time on their sites.

Researchers are now building monitoring technologies to track memes across different social platforms. But they can investigate only what they can access, and the data from visual posts on many social platforms are not made available to researchers. Additionally, techniques for studying text such as natural-language processing are far more advanced than techniques for studying images or videos. That means the research behind solutions being rolled out is disproportionately skewed toward text-based tweets, websites, or articles published via URLs and fact-checking of claims by politicians in speeches.

Although plenty of blame has been placed on the technology companies–and for legitimate reasons– they are also products of the commercial context in which they operate. No algorithmic tweak, update to the platforms' content-moderation guidelines, or regulatory fine will alone improve our information ecosystem at the level required.

Participating In the Solution

In a healthy information commons, people would still be free to express what they want–but information that is designed to mislead, incite hatred, reinforce tribalism, or cause physical harm would not be amplified by algorithms. That means it would not be allowed to trend on Twitter or in the YouTube content recommender. Nor would it be chosen to appear in Facebook feeds, Reddit searches, or top Google results.

Until this amplification problem is resolved, it is precisely our willingness to share without thinking that agents of disinformation will use as a weapon. Hence, a disordered information environment requires that every person recognize how they, too, can become a vector in the information wars and develop a set of skills to navigate communication online as well as offline.

Currently conversations about public awareness are often focused on media literacy and often with a paternalistic framing that the public simply needs to be taught how to be smarter consumers of information. Instead online users would be better taught to develop cognitive "muscles" in emotional skepticism and trained to withstand the onslaught of content designed to trigger base fears and prejudices.

Anyone who uses websites that facilitate social interaction would do well to learn how they work–and especially how algorithms determine what users see by "prioritiz[ing] posts that spark conversations and meaningful interactions between people," in the case of a January 2018 Facebook update about its rankings. I would also recommend that everyone try to buy an advertisement on Facebook at least once. The process of setting up a campaign helps to drive understanding of the granularity of information available. You can choose to target a subcategory of people as specific as women, aged between 32 and 42, who live in the Raleigh-Durham area of North Carolina, have preschoolers, have a graduate degree, are Jewish, and like Kamala Harris. The company even permits you to test these ads in environments that allow you to fail privately. These "dark ads" let organizations target posts at certain people, but they do not sit on that organization's main page. This makes it difficult for researchers or journalists to track what posts are being targeted at different groups of people, which is particularly concerning during elections.

Facebook events are another conduit for manipulation. One of the most alarming examples of foreign interference in a U.S. election was a protest that took place in Houston, Texas, yet was entirely orchestrated by trolls based in Russia. They had set up two Facebook pages that looked authentically American. One was named "Heart of Texas" and supported secession; it created an "event" for May 21, 2016, labeled "Stop Islamification of Texas." The other page, "United Muslims of America," advertised its own protest, entitled "Save Islamic Knowledge," for the exact same time and location. The result was that two groups of people came out to protest each other, while the real creators of the protest celebrated the success at amplifying existing tensions in Houston.

Another popular tactic of disinformation agents is dubbed "astroturfing." The term was initially connected to people who wrote fake reviews for products online or tried to make it appear that a fan community was larger than it really was. Now automated campaigns use bots or the sophisticated coordination of passionate supporters and paid trolls, or a combination of both, to make it appear that a person or policy has considerable grassroots support. By making certain hashtags trend on Twitter, they hope that particular messaging will get picked up by the professional media and direct the amplification to bully specific people or organizations into silence.

Understanding how each one of us is subject to such campaigns—and might unwittingly participate in them—is a crucial first step to fighting back against those who seek to upend a sense of shared reality. Perhaps most important, though, accepting how vulnerable our society is to manufactured amplification needs to be done sensibly and calmly. Fear-mongering will only fuel more conspiracy and continue to drive down trust in quality-information sources and institutions of democracy. There are no permanent solutions to weaponized narratives. Instead we need to adapt to this new normal. Just as putting on sunscreen was a habit that society developed over time and then adjusted as additional scientific research became available, building resiliency against a disordered information environment needs to be thought about in the same vein.

About the Author

Claire Wardle is director of First Draft, an organization that conducts research and leads global trainings for reporting on and countering misinformation. Her last article for Scientific American *was about the techniques of media manipulation.*

Schoolkids Are Falling Victim to Disinformation and Conspiracy Fantasies

By Melinda Wenner Moyer

When Amanda Gardner, an educator with two decades of experience, helped to start a new charter elementary and middle school outside of Seattle last year, she did not anticipate teaching students who denied that the Holocaust happened, argued that COVID is a hoax, and told their teacher that the 2020 presidential election was rigged. Yet some children insisted that these conspiracy fantasies were true. Both misinformation, which includes honest mistakes, and disinformation, which involves an intention to mislead, have had "a growing impact on students over the past 10 to 20 years," Gardner says, yet many schools do not focus on the issue. "Most high schools probably do some teaching to prevent plagiarism, but I think that's about it."

Children, it turns out, are ripe targets for fake news. Age 14 is when kids often start believing in unproven conspiratorial ideas, according to a study published in September 2021 in the *British Journal of Developmental Psychology*. Many teens also have trouble assessing the credibility of online information. In a 2016 study involving nearly 8,000 U.S. students, Stanford University researchers found that more than 80 percent of middle schoolers believed that an advertisement labeled as sponsored content was actually a news story. The researchers also found that less than 20 percent of high schoolers seriously questioned spurious claims in social media, such as a Facebook post that said images of strange-looking flowers, supposedly near the site of a nuclear power plant accident in Japan, proved that dangerous radiation levels persisted in the area. When college students in the survey looked at a Twitter post touting a poll favoring gun control, more than two thirds failed to note that the liberal anti-gun groups behind the poll could have influenced the data.

Disinformation campaigns often directly go after young users, steering them toward misleading content. A 2018 *Wall Street Journal* investigation found that YouTube's recommendation algorithm, which offers personalized suggestions about what users should watch next, is skewed to recommend videos that are more extreme and far-fetched than what the viewer started with. For instance, when researchers searched for videos using the phrase "lunar eclipse," they were steered to a video suggesting that Earth is flat. YouTube is one of the most popular social media site among teens. After Zeynep Tufekci, an associate professor at the University of North Carolina, Chapel Hill, School of Information and Library Science, spent time searching for videos on YouTube and observed what the algorithm told her to watch next, she suggested that it was "one of the most powerful radicalizing instruments of the 21st century."

One tool that schools can use to deal with this problem is called media literacy education. The idea is to teach kids how to evaluate and think critically about the messages they receive and to recognize falsehoods masquerading as truth. For children whose parents might believe conspiracy fantasies or other lies fueled by disinformation, school is the one place where they can be taught skills to evaluate such claims objectively.

Yet few American kids are receiving this instruction. Last summer Illinois became the first U.S. state to require all high school students to take a media literacy class. Thirteen other states have laws that touch on media literacy, but requirements can be as general as putting a list of resources on an education department website. A growing number of students are being taught some form of media literacy in college, but that is "way, way too late to begin this kind of instruction," says Howard Schneider, executive director of the Center for News Literacy at Stony Brook University. When he began teaching college students years ago, he found that "they came with tremendous deficits, and they were already falling into very bad habits."

Even if more students took such classes, there is profound disagreement about what those courses should teach. Certain curricula try to train students to give more weight to journalistic sources, but some researchers argue that this practice ignores the potential biases of some publications and reporters. Other courses push students to identify where information comes from and ask how the content helps those disseminating it. Overall there are very few data showing the best way to teach children how to tell fact from fiction.

Most media literacy approaches "begin to look thin when you ask, 'Can you show me the evidence?'" says Sam Wineburg, a professor of education at Stanford University, who runs the Stanford History Education Group. There are factions of educational researchers behind each method, says Renee Hobbs, director of the Media Education Lab at the University of Rhode Island, and "each group goes out of its way to diss the other." These approaches have not been compared head-to-head, and some have only small studies supporting them. Like online media sources themselves, it is hard to know which ones to trust.

News literacy is a subset of media literacy research that deals directly with the propagation of conspiracies and the ability to discern real news from fake stories. It entails a set of skills that help people judge the reliability and credibility of news and information. But as with media literacy, researchers have very different ideas about how this type of news analysis should be taught.

Some programs, such as Schneider's Stony Brook program and the nonprofit, Washington, D.C.–based News Literacy Project, teach students to discern the quality of the information in part by learning how responsible journalism works. They study how journalists pursue news, how to distinguish between different kinds of information and how to judge evidence behind reported stories. The goal, Schneider wrote in a 2007 article for *Nieman Reports*, is to shape students into "consumers who could differentiate between raw, unmediated information coursing through the Internet and independent, verified journalism."

Yet some media literacy scholars doubt the efficacy of these approaches. Hobbs, for instance, wrote a 2010 paper arguing that these methods glorify journalism, ignore its many problems, and do little to instill critical thinking skills. "All that focus on the ideals of journalism is mere propaganda if it is blind to the realities of contemporary journalism, where partisan politics and smear fests are the surest way to build audiences," she stated.

Other approaches teach students methods for evaluating the credibility of news and information sources, in part by determining the goals and incentives of those sources. They teach students to ask: Who created the content and why? And what do other sources say? But these methods are relatively new and have not been widely studied.

The lack of rigorous studies of the different approaches is indeed a major roadblock, says Paul Mihailidis, a civic media and journalism expert at Emerson College. He is the principal investigator of the Mapping Impactful Media Literacy Practices initiative, a research project supported by the National Association for Media Literacy Education. "Most of the science done is very small scale, very exploratory. It's very qualitative," he says. That is not simply because of a lack of resources, he adds. "There's also a lack of clarity about what the goals are."

For instance, in a 2017 study researchers looked at how well students who had taken Stony Brook's undergraduate course could answer certain questions a year later compared with students who had not. Students who had taken the class were more likely to correctly answer questions about the news media, such as that PBS does not rely primarily on advertising for financial support. But the study did not test how well the students could discern fake from real news, so it is hard to know how well the program inoculates students against falsehoods.

Moreover, the small amount of research that does exist has largely been conducted with college students, not the middle school or high school students who are so vulnerable to disinformation. Indeed, the various approaches that are being used in K–12 classrooms have hardly been tested at all. As part of his current research initiative, Mihailidis and his team interviewed the heads of all major organizations that are part of the National Media Literacy Alliance, which works to promote media literacy education. "We are finding, repeatedly, that many of the ways in which they support schools and teachers–resources, guidelines, best practices, etcetera–are not studied in much of a rigorous fashion," he says.

Some researchers, including Wineburg, are trying to fill in the research gaps. In a study published in 2019, Wineburg and his team compared how 10 history professors, 10 journalism fact-checkers, and 25 Stanford undergraduates evaluated websites and information on social and political issues. They found that whereas historians and students were often fooled by manipulative websites, journalism fact-checkers were not. In addition, their methods of analysis differed significantly: historians and students tried to assess the validity of websites and information by reading vertically, navigating within a site to learn more about it, but fact-checkers read laterally, opening new browser tabs for different sources and running searches to judge the original website's credibility.

Working with the Poynter Institute and the Local Media Association and with support from Google.org (a charity founded by the technology giant), Wineburg and his team have created a civic online reasoning course that teaches students to evaluate information by reading laterally. The effects so far look promising. In a field experiment involving 40,000 high school students in urban public health districts, Wineburg and his group found that students who took the class became better able to evaluate websites and the credibility of online claims, such as Facebook posts, compared with students who did not take the class.

Still, even if news literacy education teaches specific skills well, some researchers question its broader, longer-term impact. Once students learn how to evaluate websites and claims, how confident can we be that they will retain these skills and use them down the line? How sure can we be that these methods will inculcate students with skepticism about conspiracy theories and disinformation campaigns? And will these methods lead students to become civically engaged members of society? "There's always this kind of leap into 'that will make our democracy and news systems stronger.' And I don't know if that's necessarily the case," Mihailidis says.

Some research does hint that news literacy approaches could have these broader beneficial effects. In a 2017 study of 397 adults, researchers found that people who were more media-literate were less likely to endorse conspiracy theories compared with people who were less media-literate. "We can't definitely say news literacy causes you to reject conspiracy theories, but the fact that we see a positive relationship there tells us there's something to this that we need to continue to explore," says co-author Seth Ashley, an associate professor of journalism and media studies at Boise State University.

While Ashley's results are encouraging, some experts worry that a focus only on evaluating websites and news articles is too narrow. "News literacy in a lot of ways focuses on credibility and whether we know something is true or not, and that's a really important question, but that is one question," says Michelle Ciulla Lipkin, executive director of the National Association for Media Literacy Education. "Once we figure out if it's false or true, what is the other assessment and the other analyzing we need to do?" Determining credibility of the information is just the first step, she argues. Students should also be thinking about why the news is being told in a particular way, whose stories are being told and whose are not, and how the information is getting to the news consumer.

Pressing students to be skeptical about all information also may have unexpected downsides. "We think that some approaches to media literacy not only don't work but might actually backfire by increasing students' cynicism or exacerbating misunderstandings about the way news media work," says Peter Adams, senior vice president of education at the News Literacy Project. Students may begin to "read all kinds of nefarious motives into everything." Adams's concern was amplified by danah boyd (lowercase intentional), a technology scholar at Microsoft Research and founder and president of the Data & Society research institute, in a 2018 talk at the South by Southwest media conference. Boyd argued that although it is good to ask students to challenge their assumptions, "the hole that opens up, that invites people to look for new explanations, that hole can be filled in deeply problematic ways." Jordan Russell, a high school social studies teacher in Bryan, Texas, agrees. "It's very easy for students to go from healthy critical thinking to unhealthy skepticism" and the idea that everyone is lying all the time, he says.

To avoid these potential problems, Ashley advocates for broad approaches that help students develop mindsets in which they become comfortable with uncertainty. According to educational psychologist William Perry of Harvard University, students go through various stages of learning. First children are black-and-white thinkers—they think there are right answers and wrong answers. Then they develop into relativists, realizing that knowledge can be contextual. This stage can be dangerous, however. It is the one where, as Russell notes, people can come to believe there is no truth. Ashley adds that when students think everything is a lie, they also think there is no point in engaging with difficult topics.

With news literacy education, the goal is to get students to the next level, "to that place where you can start to see and appreciate the fact that the world is messy, and that's okay," Ashley says. "You have these fundamental approaches to gathering knowledge that you can accept, but you still value uncertainty, and you value ongoing debates about how the world works." Instead of driving students to apathy, the goal is to steer them toward awareness and engagement.

Schools still have a long way to go before they get there, though. One big challenge is how to expand these programs so they reach everyone, especially kids in lower-income school districts, who are much less likely to receive any news literacy instruction at all. And teachers already have so much material they have to impart—can they squeeze in more, especially if what they have to add is nuanced and complex? "[We] desperately need professional development and training and support for educators because they're not experts in the field," Adams says. "And it's the most complex and fraught and largest information landscape in human history."

In 2019 Senator Amy Klobuchar of Minnesota introduced the Digital Citizenship and Media Literacy Act into the U.S. Senate, which, if passed, would authorize $20 million to create a grant program at the Department of Education to help states develop and fund media literacy education initiatives in K–12 schools. More investment in this kind of education is critical if America's young people are going to learn how to navigate this new and constantly evolving media landscape with their wits about them. And more research is necessary to understand how to get them there. At the Center for News Literacy, Schneider plans to conduct a trial soon to determine how his course shapes the development of news literacy, civic engagement and critical thinking skills among students in middle school and high school.

But many more studies will be needed for researchers to reach a comprehensive understanding of what works and what doesn't over the long term. Education scholars need to take "an ambitious, big step forward," Schneider says. "What we're facing are transformational changes in the way we receive, process and share information. We're in the middle of the most profound revolution in 500 years."

About the Author

Melinda Wenner Moyer, a contributing editor at Scientific American, *is author of* How to Raise Kids Who Aren't Assholes: Science-Based Strategies for Better Parenting–From Tots to Teens *(G. P. Putnam & Sons, 2021).*

We Should Teach Media Literacy in Elementary School

By Prateek Puri

Nowadays, a typical news session begins with us logging on to our preferred social media website in the morning to catch up on what we missed while we slept. We quickly scroll past the memes from high-school friends or extended family, rolling our eyes at their attempts to ridicule opposing viewpoints with a few characters' worth of oversimplified, clickbait logic. After debating whether to deploy the "block content" button, we move on to consuming self-aligned content whose conclusions support our own existing views. We indulge in self-validation for a few more minutes and then log off, baffled as to how anyone could possibly ever think differently than we do.

It's a script that rose to the national spotlight during the 2016 election and one that appears to have become more and more prevalent as we near the 2018 midterms, especially recently as the nation reels over the Kavanaugh controversy and contentious DACA rulings.

We increasingly rely on social media platforms as mediums to interpret and disseminate political information. Consequently, tech giants such as Facebook and Twitter have come under close scrutiny for the ways they mediate and censor these discussions. In particular, they have been accused of providing a safe house for "fake news"–online content rife with misinformation that can lead to political hyperpolarization.

A recent troubling MIT study revealed that "fake news" diffused significantly farther, faster, deeper and more broadly than the truth, with the effect even more pronounced when regarding political news as opposed to reporting on natural disasters, finance, or science.

More worrisome, contrary to the perception that the fake news epidemic is a conception of malicious online news-bots, there is evidence that suggests the public actually *craves* fake news. The same study as mentioned above found that online bots were equally likely to propagate both false and truthful information, implying that the fake news epidemic exists because humans, not internet bots, are fueling it by favoring misinformation.

Psychologists have speculated that this phenomenon can be explained by humans' inherent need to harmonize their observations with their existing view of the world—a need to avoid what's known as cognitive dissonance. For example, Mark Whitmore, a psychologist specialized in information psychology, explains "the brain is hardwired to accept, reject, misremember or distort information based on whether it is viewed as accepting of or threatening to existing beliefs."

As a result, instead of gravitating towards well-balanced, rigorously verified news content, we have developed a diet for self-validating sensationalism, and the social media sector, controlled by a mere handful of for-profit tech firms, is happy to oblige our tastes.

The danger of online misinformation is clear. A recent study revealed that one in four Americans visited a fake news website in the preceding weeks of the 2016 election, with several observers speculating that such new sources played a substantial role in shaping the elections and manipulating voter turnout. In addition, the overabundance of information has caused many to question the integrity of some of our country's long-established institutions, such as our intelligence agencies and the media, shaking faith in the very bedrocks of our democracy.

So how can we incentivize individuals to seek accurate online content? Leading scholars are actively grappling with this question because there is still much we don't understand about the "fake news" phenomenon, but many have suggested the problem's complexity stems from the strong counter-incentive against rejecting fake information.

Processing and internalizing new information requires a considerable mental effort, especially when that information conflicts with your existing worldview. You need to assess the information, consider if it is consistent with your beliefs, and if not, restructure your belief system to accommodate the new observations. It takes vulnerability and the willingness to admit you may be wrong. In short, it takes work.

Alternatively, one could elect simply to dismiss information that isn't consistent with your existing worldview and accept the information that is. With an overwhelming amount of conflicting information available, who's to say what's actually true and what's false? If you can't tell, why not just make life easy and go with what supports your current beliefs?

So what options do we have? Many suggest that addressing the issue by reforming adult behavior is aiming too far from the source. An alternative solution is using early education to help individuals recognize these psychological pitfalls and apply critical thinking to the information they consume. Currently, there is a push in the U.S. to incorporate internet information classes into primary and secondary school curriculum. The movement, which has received bipartisan support, aims to make fact-checking seem like second nature to individuals at an early age so they will be less vulnerable to agenda-driven information sources throughout their life. While the data are still streaming in, one recent study involving 15–27 year olds revealed that media-literacy training made individuals less likely to believe a demonstrably false claim, even when the statement was aligned with their existing political point of view.

Legislation centered on this idea has already been passed in states such as Washington, Connecticut, Rhode Island, and New Mexico, with some now offering media literacy courses as electives at select public schools.

Primary and secondary school are supposed to be supplying students with the skills they need to develop into productive, informed members of our society. As our society evolves, the curriculum we are teaching our students need to evolve as well. Schools have partly recognized this by incorporating programming and computer science classes into curricula to match our tech-hungry society, but we need to go further and also instruct our youth on how to properly consume and disseminate online information.

We need to have a lot of difficult conversations in order to resolve the issues we are facing as a society, and the only way these conversations will be productive and enduring is if we all can agree on the facts. Right now, with Americans believing more than 40 percent of the news they see is fake, we aren't quite there as a society, but that doesn't mean we can't be. The internet is an amazing tool, but to use it most effectively we have to embrace its benefits while also understanding the ways in which it makes us vulnerable. If students are still learning dated practices such as cursive writing in school, shouldn't they be learning how to navigate and consume the internet responsibly as well?

If you would like to support movements similar to the ones mentioned here, contact your local school board officer today or get involved media literacy organizations such as such as Media Literacy Now and the Digital Citizenship Institute.

About the Author

Prateek Puri is a National Science Foundation Graduate Research fellow studying atomic physics at the University of California, Los Angeles.

The Psychology of Fact-Checking

By Stephen J. Ceci and Wendy M. Williams

Distortions and outright lies by politicians and pundits have become so common that major news outlets like the Associated Press, CNN, BBC, Fox News, and the *Washington Post* routinely assign journalists and fact-checkers to verify claims made during stump speeches and press briefings. The motivation to uncover falsehoods and misleading statements taken out of context is laudable. But when it comes to real-world complexities, the trouble is that people often see different things when looking at the same event, a phenomenon repeatedly documented by psychologists.

Laboratory studies reveal that, when shown a video of a group of protesters, people see either a peaceful protest or an unruly mob blocking pedestrian access, depending on their sociopolitical beliefs. The world outside the lab shows similar biased perception: For example, 68 percent of Republicans consider the videotaped demonstrations in Portland, Ore., Kenosha, Wisc., and New York City to be riots, versus only 30 percent of Democrats, according to a Fox News poll released in September. Journalists and fact-checkers are human beings subject to the same psychological biases as everyone else—and their analyses of what constitute "facts" is affected by their own political and ideological values, resulting in what psychologists term *selective perception*.

Consider the claim that during an interview with the progressive activist Ady Barkan, Joe Biden stated he favors defunding the police. This allegation has been dismissed as taken out of context and consequently false by some journalists and fact-checkers (e.g., *Politifact's* Jon Greenberg), and CNN's Facts First argued that Biden had denied he favored defunding in comments that were not included in the published interview with Barkan. However, others argued Biden's statement about supporting "redirecting" funds to other agencies was a clear acknowledgment of his support of decreased funding for police.

For example, Evie Fordham of Fox News states that redirecting funds from the police is the only context in which Biden's "yes, absolutely" answer to Barkan's question can be understood, in her words: "despite the fact that Barkan did not say 'for police' at the end of the question, the context of the original exchange made clear that Barkan was talking about redirecting police funding."). The result is a massive disagreement, with many journalists and fact-checkers arguing that Biden's critics did indeed take his statement out of context, and he did not intend to support a redirection of funds away from law enforcement, as fact-checkers Hope Yen at the Associated Press and the BBC's Jake Horton contended, whereas CNN cited a Biden statement from early June in which he said it makes sense for some local communities to reduce police funding. In examining the evidence that each side invoked, it is possible to make a case for both positions.

The same is true of the allegation that in the aftermath of Heather Heyer's death in Charlottesville, Va., in 2017, Trump said there were "fine people" among protestors and counterprotestors, a statement generally interpreted by liberal fact-checkers and journalists as referring to fine people among the white supremacists and Neo-Nazis but disputed by conservative journalists.

Even when the original facts may tilt in the direction of journalists' and fact-checker's claims, they may be too ambiguous to justify the unequivocal headlines that have appeared: ("AP Fact Check: Trump distorts record; BLM falsely accused").

Fact-checkers' decisions have significant consequences for debates about fake news that cannot be overstated. Researchers have studied the cascading cognitive effects of misinformation, and their findings are relevant to current concerns about fake news and to the limitations of fact-checking. Misinformation can be insidious; it can seep into the unconscious mind and influence beliefs and behaviors long after we have forgotten its source or the evidence invoked to support it. Under laboratory conditions, a selection of objective facts and complete fabrications can be presented, and researchers can then examine the spread of misinformation about these facts and whether and how this spread results in false beliefs.

Unlike a pristine laboratory setting, however, the world of politics is messy, and there can be deep disagreements about the facts themselves, as the above contradictory claims illustrate. When it comes to partisan fact-checking about complex issues–which describes much of the fact-checking that takes place in the context of political news–the truth as stated is often the subjective opinion of people with shared political views.

One path to a solution is "adversarial fact-checking." Fact-checking is often done by teams of two or more journalists rather than by a single person. We propose that political claims continue to be aggressively fact-checked, but by teams of individuals with diverse sociopolitical views; for example, by pairing fact-checkers from major liberal and conservative news sources. This would add little, if any, cost. The media should abandon fact-checkers' pretext of objectivity and political disinterest and instead acknowledge their sociopolitical leanings in much the way that NPR tries to pit pro and con points of view in political coverage.

Research underscores that fact-checkers' personal biases influence both their choice of which statements to analyze and their determination of accuracy. Let diverse fact-checkers work as members of an adversarial team, much like two sides in arbitration. Fact-checkers are human beings who live in the real world, rather than in a sociopolitical monastery. Let's abandon the pretense of objectivity and design a system of adversarial fact-checking that places the evidence for competing claims front and center.

Exposure to contrasting views sometimes happens when a counterclaim appears days or weeks later or an independent fact-checker like PolitiFact requests a retraction, but the key to better cognitive reasoning outcomes is for both sides' claims to appear simultaneously in the very same report. This would minimize the creation of false beliefs that emerge as a consequence of exposure to only one side. When adversarial fact-checking leads to unresolvable disagreements among team members, readers will be better able to judge how persuasive each side's argument is and arrive at a more informed conclusion than they would if only one side's evidence is presented.

It would be a valuable antidote to the tendency of Americans to base their views on sources solely within their "bubble." Such an adversarial arrangement challenges the presumption that there can be no doubt about the validity of fact-checkers' conclusions, as implied by CNN's Facts First feature: "CNN holds elected officials and candidates accountable by pointing out what's true and what's not," as if determining the truth is somehow a psychologically straightforward process.

Having each side's fact-checkers checked by the other side's fact-checkers could lead to an infinite regress toward an uncertain truth. But this is preferable to belief in a truth that may not exist. Adversarial fact-checkers would debate the same "evidence" and ensure a balanced presentation of the facts. This may not guarantee that fact-checkers will agree or even that readers will discern the truth. But it will reveal the sometimes-tenuous nature of fact-checkers' claims and the psychological context in which human cognition unfolds–and this would be a meaningful barrier to the spread of fake news and the creation of false beliefs among voters.

About the Authors

Stephen J. Ceci is a professor of development psychology at Cornell University

Wendy M. Williams is a professor of human development at Cornell University.

(Dis)trust in Science

By Gleb Tsipursky

Dozens of infants and children in Romania died recently in a major measles outbreak, a result of prominent celebrities campaigning against vaccination. This trend parallels that of Europe as a whole, which suffered a 400 percent increase in measles cases from 2016 to 2017. Unvaccinated Americans traveling to the World Cup may well bring the disease back to the U.S.

Of course, we don't need to go to Europe to catch measles. Kansas just experienced its worst outbreak in decades. Children and adults in a few unvaccinated families were key to this widespread outbreak. Just as in Romania, parents in the U.S. are fooled by the false claim that vaccines cause autism. This belief has spread widely across the U.S. and leads to a host of problems.

Measles was practically eliminated in the U.S. by 2000. However, in recent years outbreaks of measles have been on the rise, driven by parents failing to vaccinate their children in a number of communities. We should be especially concerned because [Trump] has frequently expressed the false view that vaccines cause autism, and his administration has pushed against funding science-based policies at the Centers for Disease Control.

These illnesses and deaths are one among many terrible consequences of the crisis of trust suffered by our institutions in recent years. While headlines focus on declining trust in the media and the government, science and academia are not immune to this crisis of confidence, and the results can be deadly.

Consider that in 2006, 41 percent of respondents in a nationwide poll expressed "a lot of confidence" in higher education. Less than 10 years later, in 2014, only 14 percent of those surveyed showed "a great deal of confidence" in academia.

What about science as distinct from academia? Polling shows that the number of people who believe that science has "made life more difficult" increased by 50 percent from 2009 to 2015.

According to a 2017 survey, only 35 percent of respondents have "a lot" of trust in scientists; the number of people who do "not at all" trust scientists increased by over 50 percent from a similar poll conducted in December 2013.

This crumbling of trust in science and academia forms part of a broader pattern, what Tom Nichols called *The Death of Expertise* in his 2017 book. Growing numbers of people claim their personal opinions hold equal weight to the opinions of experts.

Should We Trust Scientific Experts?

While we can all agree that we do not want people to get sick, what is the underlying basis for the idea that the opinions of experts—including scientists—deserve more trust than the average person in evaluating the truth of reality?

The term "expert" refers to someone who has extensive familiarity with a specific area, as shown by commonly recognized credentials such as a certification, an academic degree, publication of a book, years of experience in a field, or another way that a reasonable person may recognize an "expert." Experts are able to draw on their substantial body of knowledge and experience to provide an opinion, often expressed as "expert analysis."

That doesn't mean an expert opinion will always be right: it's simply much more likely to be right than the opinion of a non-expert. The underlying principle here is probabilistic thinking, our ability to predict the truth of current and future reality based on limited information. Thus, a scientist studying autism would be much more likely to predict accurately the consequences of vaccinations than someone who has spent 10 hours googling "vaccines and autism" online.

This greater likelihood of experts being correct does not at all mean we should always defer to experts. First, research shows that experts do best in evaluating reality in environments that are relatively stable over time and thus predictable, and also when the experts have a chance to learn about the predictable aspects of this environment. Second, other research suggests that ideological biases can have a strongly negative impact on the ability of experts to make accurate evaluations. Third, material motivations can sway experts to conduct an analysis favorable to their financial sponsor.

However, while individual scientists may make mistakes, it is incredibly rare for the scientific consensus as a whole to be wrong. Scientists get rewarded in money and reputation for finding fault with statements about reality made by other scientists. Thus, for the large majority of them to agree on something–for there to be a scientific consensus–is a clear indicator that whatever they agree on reflects reality accurately.

The Internet is for . . . Misinformation

The rise of the Internet and, more recently, social media is key to explaining the declining public confidence in expert opinion.

Before the Internet, the information accessible to the general public about any given topic usually came from experts. For instance, scientific experts on autism were invited to talk on this topic on mainstream media, large publishers published books by the same experts, and they wrote encyclopedia articles on this topic.

The Internet has enabled anyone to be a publisher of content, connecting people around the world with any and all sources of information. On the one hand, this freedom is empowering and liberating, with Wikipedia a great example of a highly curated source on the vast majority of subjects. On the other, anyone can publish a blog piece making false claims about links between vaccines and autism. If they are skilled at search engine optimization, or have money to invest in advertising, they can get their message spread widely.

Unfortunately, research shows that people lack the skills for differentiating misinformation from true information. This lack of skills has clear real-world effects: just consider that U.S. adults believed 75 percent of fake news stories about the 2016 U.S. presidential election. The more often someone sees a piece of misinformation, the more likely they are to believe it.

Blogs with falsehoods are bad enough, but the rise of social media made the situation even worse. Most people reshare news stories without reading the actual article, judging the quality of the story by the headline and image alone. No wonder that research indicates that misinformation spreads as much as 10 times faster and further on social media than true information. After all, the creator of a fake news item is free to devise the most appealing headline and image, while credible sources of information have to stick to factual headlines and images.

These problems result from the train wreck of human thought processes meeting the Internet. We all suffer from a series of thinking errors such as confirmation bias, our tendency to look for and interpret information in ways that conform to our beliefs.

Before the Internet, we got our information from sources such as mainstream media and encyclopedias, which curated the information for us to ensure it came from experts, minimizing the problem of confirmation bias. Now, the lack of curation means thinking errors are causing us to choose information that fits our intuitions and preferences, as opposed to the facts. Moreover, some unscrupulous foreign actors–such as the Russian government–and domestic politicians use misinformation as a tool to influence public discourse and public policy.

The large gaps between what scientists and the public believe about issues such as climate change, evolution, GMOs, and vaccination exemplify the problems caused by misinformation and lack of trust in science. Such mistrust results in great harm to our society, from outbreaks of preventable diseases to highly damaging public policies.

What Can We Do?

Fortunately, there are proactive steps we can take to address the crisis of trust in science and academia.

For example, we can uplift the role of science in our society. The March for Science movement is a great example of this effort. First held on Earth Day in 2017 and repeated in 2018, this effort involves people rallying in the streets to celebrate science and push for evidence-based policies. Another example is the Scholars Strategy Network, an effort to support scholars in popularizing their research for a broad audience and connecting scholars to policy makers.

We can also fight the scourge of misinformation. Many world governments are taking steps to combat falsehoods. While the U.S. federal government has dropped the ball on this problem, a number of states passed bipartisan efforts promoting media literacy. Likewise, many nongovernmental groups are pursuing a variety of efforts to fight misinformation.

The Pro-Truth Pledge combines the struggle against misinformation with science advocacy. Founded by a group of behavioral science experts (including myself) and concerned citizens, the pledge calls on public figures, organizations, and private citizens to commit to 12 behaviors listed on the pledge website that research in behavioral science show correlate with truthfulness. Signers are held accountable through a crowd-sourced reporting and evaluation mechanism while getting reputational rewards because of their commitment. The scientific consensus serves as a key measure of credibility, and the pledge encourages pledge-takers to recognize the opinions of experts as more likely to be true when the facts are disputed.

More than 500 politicians took the pledge, including state legislators Eric Nelson (Pa.) and Ogden Driskell (Wyo.), and members of U.S. Congress Beto O'Rourke (Texas) and Marcia Fudge (Ohio). Two research studies at Ohio State University have demonstrated with a strong statistical significance the effectiveness of the pledge in changing the behavior of pledge-takers to be more truthful. Thus, taking the pledge yourself and encouraging people you know and your elected representatives to take the pledge is an easy action to both fight misinformation and promote science.

I have a dream that, one day, children will not be getting sick with measles because their parents put their trust in a random blogger instead of extensive scientific studies. I have a dream that schools will be teaching media literacy, and people will know how to evaluate the firehose of information coming their way. I have a dream that we will all know that we suffer from thinking errors and watch out for confirmation bias and other problems. I have a dream that the quickly growing distrust of experts and science will seem like a bad dream. I have a dream that our grandchildren will find it hard to believe our present reality when we tell them stories about the bad old days.

To live these dreams requires all of us who care about truth and science to act now, before we fall further down the slippery slope. Our information ecosystem and credibility mechanisms are broken. Only a third of Americans trust scientists and most people can't tell the difference between truth and falsehood online. The lack of trust in science—and the excessive trust in persuasive purveyors of misinformation—is perhaps the biggest threat to our society right now. If we don't turn back from the brink, our future will not be a dream: it will be a nightmare.

About the Author

Gleb Tsipursky is a behavioral scientist, CEO of the future-proofing consultancy Disaster Avoidance Experts and author of Returning to the Office and Leading Hybrid and Remote Teams: A Manual on Benchmarking to Best Practices for Competitive Advantage.

GLOSSARY

algorithm A set of rules in software that guide information processing and calculations.

alienation The sensation of being estranged from or rejected by society.

bot Short for robot; internet software designed to imitate human behavior.

cognitive dissonance In psychology, the state of holding conflicting or inconsistent ideas.

disenfranchisement The loss of one's rights as a citizen.

dissemination Spread, distribution, diffusion.

implausible Not believable, probable, or acceptable.

neural network A computer network meant to approximate how the human brain works.

objectivity The ability to process facts or ideas separate from one's own feelings or opinions.

polarization The division of people into groups holding opposite opinions.

sensationalism The publishing of extraordinary or exaggerated events to attract readers.

veracity Truthfulness, trustworthiness, accuracy, correctness.

visceral Relating to the emotions and feelings rather than rational thought.

zealot Someone passionately devoted to an idea or cause, often used negatively.

FURTHER INFORMATION

DelViscio, Jeffrey. "A Nixon Deepfake, a 'Moon Disaster' Speech and an Information Ecosystem at Risk," *Scientific American*, 20 July 2020, https://www.scientificamerican.com/article/a-nixon-deepfake-a-moon-disaster-speech-and-an-information-ecosystem-at-risk1/

Hiar, Corbin. "Google Bans Ads That Spread Climate Misinformation," *Scientific American*, 8 October 2021, https://www.scientificamerican.com/article/google-bans-ads-that-spread-climate-misinformation/

Hiar, Corbin. "Twitter Bots Are a Major Source of Climate Disinformation," *Scientific American*, 22 January 2021, https://www.scientificamerican.com/article/twitter-bots-are-a-major-source-of-climate-disinformation/

Pelletier, Justin. "Russian Cyberattacks against the U.S. Could Focus on Disinformation," *Scientific American*, 28 January 2022, https://www.scientificamerican.com/article/russian-cyberattacks-against-the-u-s-could-focus-on-disinformation/

Pennycock, Gordon. "Shifting Attention to Accuracy Can Reduce Misinformation Online," *Nature* 17 March 2021, https://www.nature.com/articles/s41586-021-03344-2

Schwartz, Jen. "When a Journalist Becomes a Disinformation Agent," Scientific American 12 October 2020, https://www.scientificamerican.com/article/when-a-journalist-becomes-a-disinformation-agent/

CITATIONS

1.1 Three Historical Examples of "Fake News" by Krystal D'Costa (December 1, 2016); 1.2 The Deep Roots of Fake News by John Horgan (February 1, 2019); 1.3 Unlimited Information Is Transforming Society by Naomi Oreskes, Erik M. Conway (September 1, 2020); 1.4 To Understand How Science Denial Works, Look to History by Naomi Oreskes (December 1, 2020); 1.5 How the Pandemic Remade Science Journalism by Tanya Lewis (March 1, 2022); 1.6 COVID Has Created a Perfect Storm for Fringe Science by David Robert Grimes (April 26, 2021); 2.1 People Drawn to Conspiracy Theories Share a Cluster of Psychological Features by Melinda Wenner Moyer (March 1, 2019); 2.2 Cognitive Ability and Vulnerability to Fake News by David Z. Hambrick, Madeline Marquardt (February 6, 2018); 2.3 How Disinformation Hacks Your Brain by Brett Beasley (December 26, 2019); 2.5 Why Are Deepfakes So Effective? by Martijn Rasser (August 14, 2019); 2.6 AI-Generated Deepfakes and the Challenge of Detection by Siwei Lyu (July 20, 2020); 3.1 You Can't Handle the Truth–at Least on Twitter by Larry Greenemeier (March 8, 2018); 3.2 How Facebook Hinders Misinformation Research by Laura Edelson, Damon McCoy (September 22, 2021); 3.3 Russia's Information War Is Being Waged on Social Media Platforms by Sophie Bushwick (March 8, 2022); 3.4 YouTube's Plan to Showcase Credible Health Information Is Flawed, Experts Warn by Grant Currin (August 27, 2021); 3.5 How Fake News Goes Viral–Here's the Math by Madhusree Mukerjee (July 14, 2017); 3.6 Information Overload Helps Fake News Spread, and Social Media Knows It by Filippo Menczer, Thomas Hills (December 1, 2020); 4.1 How 9/11 Ushered in a New Era of Conspiracy Theories by Jason Stanley (September 10, 2021); 4.2 Personality Type, as well as Politics, Predicts Who Shares Fake News by Asher Lawson, Hemant Kakkar (November 12, 2021); 4.3 Liberals and Conservatives Are Both Susceptible to Fake News, but for Different Reasons by Scott Barry Kaufman (February 14, 2019); 4.4 Fake News Web Sites May Not Have a Major Effect on Elections by Karen Weintraub (March 2, 2020); 4.5 Russian Misinformation Seeks to Confound, Not Convince by David Robert Grimes (March 28, 2022); 4.6 Clicks, Lies and Videotape by Brooke Borel (October 1, 2018); 5.1 Misinformation Has Created a New World Disorder by Claire Wardle (September 1, 2019); 5.2 Schoolkids Are Falling Victim to Disinformation and Conspiracy Fantasies by Melinda Wenner Moyer (February 1, 2022); 5.3 We Should Teach Media Literacy in Elementary School by Prateek Puri (November 7, 2018); 5.4 The Psychology of Fact-Checking by Stephen J. Ceci, Wendy M. Williams (October 25, 2020); 5.5 (Dis)trust in Science by Gleb Tsipursky (July 5, 2018)

Each author biography was accurate at the time the article was originally published.

INDEX

A

Ailes, Roger, 12
Associated Press, 146–147

B

BBC, 146–147
Biden, Joe, 112, 146–147
Brexit, 110, 126
Bush, George W., 95–96
Buzzfeed, 45, 113, 117

C

Carlson, Tucker, 109
Catholic Church, 8–9
Civil War, U.S., 12
climate change, 13, 25–26, 37, 41, 43, 86, 126–127, 153
CNN, 38, 146–147, 149
Constantine, Emperor, 8–10
COVID-19, 25, 28–30, 32–34, 65, 73–74, 83, 98, 110–111, 134

D

Death of Expertise, The, 151
deepfakes, 53–59, 117–119, 122
Duterte, Rodrigo, 126

E

Eisenhower, Dwight, 19

F

Facebook, 24, 26, 45, 62–63, 65–67, 69–70, 74, 80, 83, 87, 93, 101, 107, 118, 122–123, 125, 127, 130–132, 134, 138, 142
Fox News, 12, 29, 109, 146–147
Franklin, Benjamin, 9–10, 12, 16

I

Instagram, 24, 67, 87, 127, 130
Iraq War, 95–96

L

Lepore, Jill, 11–14

M

memes, 78–82, 85, 88, 91–92, 127, 129–130, 142
Memes to Movements, 130
Merchants of Doubt, 26

N

Nazis, 12, 20, 96

New Yorker, 13

New York Sun, 10

New York Times, 12

Nixon, Richard, 12

O

Obama, Barack, 101, 113, 116–118, 120, 123

P

PBS, 137

Philippines, 126

ProPublica, 14

R

Reagan, Ronald, 12, 110

Roosevelt, Franklin, 12

Russia, 39, 41, 45, 65, 69–72, 109–112, 130, 132

S

Spanish-American War, 17

Suspicious Minds: Why We Believe in Conspiracy Theories, 44

T

These Truths: A History of the United States, 11–14

TikTok, 75

tobacco industry, 25–26, 109

Trump, Donald, 11, 13–14, 28–29, 38, 41, 43–45, 50–51, 63, 95–96, 99, 101–102, 104, 106, 113, 116–118, 129–130, 147, 150

Twitter, 54, 61–63, 69, 74, 80–81, 86–87, 89–93, 107, 118, 122, 125, 130–131, 133–134, 142

V

Vietnam War, 12

W

Wall Street Journal, 135

Washington Post, 50, 95, 146

World War I, 18

World War II, 18, 21, 25

Y

YouTube, 69–70, 73–76, 87, 131, 135